PRESCRIBING

LEADERSHIP

in

HEALTHCARE

To Lisa,

Lead Every Day!

Praise for *Prescribing Leadership in Healthcare*

"Professor Bennett has a thorough and compelling leadership process that he shares in *Prescribing Leadership in Healthcare*. The lessons and practices he shares will make us all better leaders and most importantly, will directly benefit those patients and families we serve."
David Feinberg, President and CEO, Geisinger Health

"This is one of the best and most powerful leadership books I have read. It is a concise and practical roadmap for developing leaders. Bennett defines leadership as a process rather than a position, with leaders being both "born and made". He relates leadership to sports and makes a strong parallel to professional athletes who must train themselves to become even better.

The healthcare industry is facing dynamic change and sorely needs dynamic leaders to facilitate transformation. To develop yourself to be that kind of leader, one needs self-assessment, mentoring and practice. Prescribing Leadership in Healthcare is an excellent tool to hone God-given leadership skills and also help "make" leaders who have aptitude and desire. Bennett prescribes a process for daily leadership exercise. I believe he has found an elixir for making all of us better leaders.

I highly recommend you read and highlight this book. The book's title, *Prescribing Leadership in Healthcare* says it all. Get the prescription and take it soon if you want to further your career and find success as a healthcare leader. This book is a treasure."
Jim Mattes, President & CEO, Grande Ronde Hospital
AHA's Most Wired – Small and Rural Hospital, 2017 & 2016

"Bryan Bennett is one of those authors and leaders who is exceptionally inspiring to many of us every day. He is very gifted and persistent and visionary. In many ways his inspirational leadership and remarkable personal strengths remind me of certain other mentors and leaders I've had that have inspired me. I highly recommend hearing Bennett speak and reading and following his leadership book. He is a remarkable person. The world needs more people like Bryan Bennett."
Scott Becker, Publisher, Becker's Hospital Review

"Hospitals are undertaking a profound digital transformation. Modernizing a system that emerged from pagers, print/fax/scan and kludgy EHRs simply cannot succeed without solid and knowledgeable leaders. In *Prescribing Leadership in Healthcare*, Mr. Bennett draws on his journey to becoming a leader as well as interviews with some of the most prominent executives in healthcare to map out the requisite traits, challenges, and technological trends such as analytics, EHRs and population health, that healthcare leaders and the industry needs. He also shares practicable advice for developing, living and practicing a leadership vision. Packed with lively and relatable sports analogies, *Prescribing Leadership in Healthcare* is a book readers will want to come back to again and again."
Tom Sullivan, Editor-in-Chief, Healthcare IT News

"*Prescribing Leadership in Healthcare* is just that. A prescription in best practices that early careerist and seasoned professionals could lean on in today's shifting healthcare environment. The analogies were seamless and clearly portrayed with relatable content. From Self-Reflection to Mentoring, this book was a quick read with potent content. There were many applicable examples and a byproduct of this read spurred an internal conversation how I too could be a better leader. In a profession with many internal and external influences, it's refreshing to have a book that pauses time just long enough to fan some flames of creatively. Well done."
Victor Jackson, CEO, Vibra Specialty Hospital of Portland

"*Prescribing Leadership in Healthcare* is a comprehensive view of the many factors that affect leaders in healthcare and their approach to problem solving from a proactive approach. He addresses many viewpoints that result in a single viewpoint. That viewpoint is that without effective leadership, you are bound to fail! Professor Bennett's work should be a must read for anyone aspiring towards leadership in a healthcare position. I fully recommend this read."
Gary Richberg, Administrator, Pacific Rim Outpatient Surgery Center

"Professor Bennett does an excellent job providing the reader with deep healthcare leadership tactics and insight to help healthcare managers become more effective in this era of rapid change."
Kenneth Waller, CEO, Amistad Community Health

"Healthcare leaders don't need a prescription to get insight from Bryan Bennett's book. His recommended innate qualities of empathy and humility provide a solid platform for self-reflection and leadership growth. Bennett encourages healthcare leaders to use stories and social media channels to increase brand awareness and trust with constituents. Practicing what he preaches, Bennett ends each chapter ends with a "Tale from the Leadership Front" which authentically illustrates the concepts discussed. My personal favorite is "Leadership Lessons from a Man in a Bow Tie."
Michelle Kilbourne, Chair, Business Programs, Judson University

PRESCRIBING

LEADERSHIP

in

HEALTHCARE

Curing the Challenges Facing
Today's Healthcare Leaders

By J. Bryan Bennett

Healthcare Center
of Excellence, LLC.

Prescribing Leadership in Healthcare:
Curing the Challenges Facing Today's Healthcare Leaders

ISBN-13: 978-1546597223
ISBN-10: 1546597220

Published by:

Healthcare Center of Excellence, LLC
Buffalo Grove, IL 60089

Email: prescribing@healthcarecoe.org
Website: http://www.healthcarecoe.org
Twitter: @healthcarecoe @jbryanbennett

PRINTED IN THE UNITED STATES OF AMERICA

I dedicate this book to my children, Bryanna and Alex. I am so proud of the people you have grown to become. Each of you inspires me in different ways. I pray that my work encourages you to continue your writing and writing-related studies. Remember to do what you are passionate about and you will always be happy.

Acknowledgements

There are always a lot of people behind creating a work such as this. Many have graciously contributed their thoughts, insights and experiences into the development of the concepts presented in this book as well as how they have implemented them in their lives. This would not have been possible without their help.

I would first like to thank all of the healthcare executives, business executives, athletes and coaches who gave of their time for interviews for this book. It was great receiving your insights on leadership and how you have prepared for your professional journeys. I would especially like to thank Dr. Toby Cosgrove from the Cleveland Clinic who was one of the first executives to agree to an interview. The more we communicate and the more I hear him speak at conferences, the more I realize what a special leader he is.

I would also like to thank Dr. Michelle Kilbourne and the staff at Judson University. Dr. Kilbourne was always open to discussing and providing candid feedback on my leadership concepts. My teaching and mentoring in the school's now top-20 Organizational Leadership program she helped build, challenged how I thought about leadership and helped me develop my personal leadership development philosophy. I want to also express my appreciation to my former leadership students who previewed the leadership concepts I was developing for the book. Their feedback helped me better articulate and present the concepts.

I want to also express my gratitude to Scott Becker, from Becker's Healthcare, for inviting me to attend and now speak at their healthcare conferences. His invitations provided access to the executives I needed to meet for the book. In fact, almost half of the healthcare executive interviewed were met at one of their conferences.

I have to also thank the "finishers", Danita Ayers, Tom Byrne, Marilyn Davis, Karen DeGrasse and Carol West. These are the people who helped me finish the book by reviewing and editing the book content or adding their perspective on the cover design.

Finally, I am indebted to my parents for providing me daily examples of great leadership – in very different ways. My mother was a director at a large insurance company and managed a staff of 150 people. We had numerous discussions about business and leading people over the years which I will always cherish. It was my father's example though of servant-leadership that has stuck with my brothers and me the most. He did everything he could to provide for our family, even if it meant working 3 or 4 low paying jobs to make sure all four of us received quality, private-school educations. His work ethic and acceptance of doing what was necessary is what has helped make me into the leader I am today. I appreciate everyone I come in contact with no matter their position. Although my parents may no longer be with me physically, I know they are here spiritually. The lifetime of learnings from them are with me throughout my life and I hope to pass these lessons along to my children.

Table of Contents

Foreword

By Chris Van Gorder

As a health care leader, I'm often asked how I got to where I am today. My usual answer is that I was fortunate – somehow, I managed to "fall up." But that's really only part of the story.

As Professor Bennett points out in the pages that follow, leadership is a process. For me it's a process that is never-ending. And once I was able to embrace it, the door opened to my becoming who I am today and who I'll be five years from now.

Leadership is an accumulation of all you learn and put into practice along your own personal journey. In my case, falling "up," doesn't mean there was no falling "down." Some of my greatest leadership lessons, in fact, were learned from mistakes I made along the way or from those I observed in others. Leadership is an evolution of ideas and principles and actions, and every leadership journey is unique and personal. Your experiences and learnings will be different than mine and different from others who are reading this book.

For example, I consider myself to be a front-line leader:

- I'm energized by spending time with my front-line managers and employees, and I do so as often as possible.

- I consider nearly every moment a teaching moment and I've found the best ways to teach are through personal, experiential stories.

- I make a point of answering every email I receive, from anyone, within 24 hours. For me it's a common courtesy, and sometimes the best way to stay connected to my front-lines.

- Every morning, every day of the year, I personally curate the top news stories of the day in health care, leadership and other areas I find interesting. I share these with my management team and anyone who asks to be on the list. This gives me a reason to directly communicate every day. In turn, those on the list learn more about our industry and it sometimes leads to very valuable conversations.

These are just some elements of my own leadership style, and I live and practice them every day. But my style is not for everyone, and it may not be yours. As you go through the leadership process, it's important to apply the lessons you learn to your own individual style, strengths and principles. No matter which approach you take to leadership, it's important to be authentic to who you are.

As you embark or continue on your own leadership journey – through this book and, I'm sure, many others – I applaud you for having the courage to always take that next step. At its core, leadership is both an external and internal exercise. To be a better leader of others, we must first be brutally honest with ourselves.

The world today is full of "leaders" who fail to demonstrate the courage, honor and commitment it takes to truly lead. As Professor Bennett describes, they are leaders by title and not by action.

Thank you for daring to be different.

Chris Van Gorder
President and CEO
Scripps Health

Chapter One -
Leadership is a Process – Not a Skill

"Outstanding leaders go out of their way to
boost the self-esteem of their personnel.
If people believe in themselves,
it's amazing what they can accomplish."
- Sam Walton, Founder, Wal-Mart

We are facing a leadership crisis which impacts all aspects of our lives. It affects us in healthcare, government, business, education and in the church. Lack of leadership is shown when a person in a leadership position puts their own needs or personal agenda ahead of those they are charged to lead. Just because someone is in a leadership position does not make them a leader. You can be in a leadership position (supervisor, manager, director, executive, etc.) and not have any leadership abilities. This is called Positional Leadership and occurs when someone has some position of authority but is not practicing any form of leadership. These people are not usually very effective at what they do and only accomplish what they do because of their authority. They were probably promoted to their position because they did their job well at a lower level, but little evaluation was given to their potential for leadership. The better word to describe them is manager, not leader. We have all known people who fall into this category and, unfortunately, many of us may have worked for them.

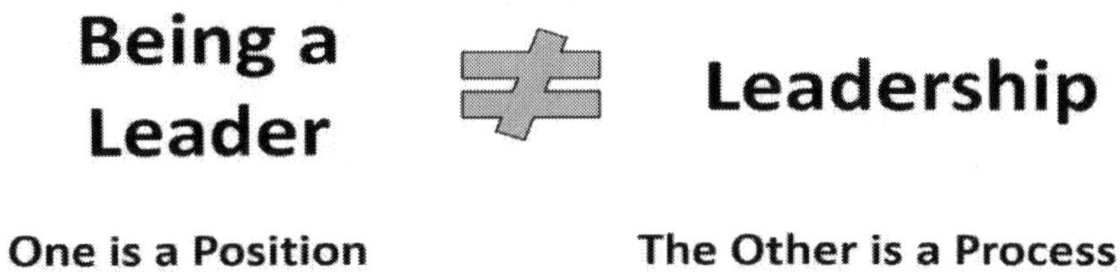

Being a Leader Leadership

One is a Position   The Other is a Process

Figure 1: Being a Leader Does Not Equal Leadership

For purposes of this book, leadership is defined as:

"A process by which an individual or organization directs and inspires a team or organization to reach a goal or follow a vision in a particular environment."

A further examination of this definition reveals:

- A process – Leadership is not a skill. It is a process that must be worked at daily for a person to become a better leader.

- Individual or organization – There are many individuals who are leaders, but an organization can also be a leader. For instance, Apple has been a leader in several technology areas for years, as well as Amazon in online retailing. Their competitors follow them, copy them and try to pass them in the marketplace.

- Directs and inspires – There are leaders who are good at directing people but not very inspirational, as well as leaders who are very inspirational but couldn't properly direct a team to cross the street with a green light. A favorite analogy is that of a baseball centerfielder running into the wall to make the catch for his team. He realizes that he might hurt himself (and many have), but he believes that helping his team win the game is more important than his personal safety. A leader must inspire people to willingly want to 'go to the wall' for the team because they may have to someday. Good leadership will help them feel good about making that choice.

- Team or organization – These are the followers in the equation. The team is the immediate staff or project team and the organization is the entire company.

- Reach a goal or follow a vision – The leader must have a specific goal for the team to achieve whether it be a sales or income goal, technology implementation or cultural change. Whatever it is, in addition to being specific, it should be measurable and have a defined time period.

- Environment – This represents the area that is largely out of the leader's control. It could be the industry, government regulations or other changes impacting the organization.

As previously mentioned, true leadership is a process that must be practiced every day to be effective. It's like a maintenance drug for high blood pressure that must be taken daily to avoid potentially dire consequences. It's like athletes, amateur or professional, who continually works hard to improve their already exceptional abilities in order to become better and more competitive. It is the same way any other professional works to become better, including:

- Physicians
- Musicians & Singers
- Artists
- Professors

This process leads to what is called **Professional Leadership**, which is a personalized, continuously-improving leadership development process based on innate qualities, personality and abilities that is practiced every day incorporating regular reflection and coaching.

The Great Leadership Debate

The great debate about leadership is whether leaders are born or made. The correct answer is "Yes." Some people have certain innate qualities that gives them a high potential for leadership (born). They can still become better leaders though through training. On the other hand, others without all of the innate qualities can become better leaders through training (made). Keep in mind that not everyone will be a good leader which is logical because society couldn't exist if everyone was a leader.

Based on research, interviews and self-reflection, the innate leadership qualities are identified as:

- Humility – putting the needs of others ahead of their own
- Empathy – knowing how to get things done through people
- Vision – the ability to see things others don't see or before others see them
- Risk-Taking – comfort with being out front and charting new territory

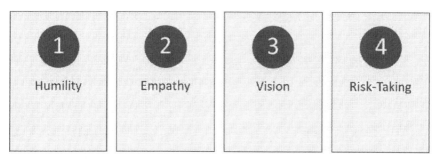

Figure 2: The Innate Leadership Qualities

Humility is the recognition of one's own importance or standing. It is the self-awareness that you are no better than the person next to you or across from you. Sometimes known as modesty, humble people make everyone feel special. Humility is the quality that is most natural. It can be learned to a certain degree, but authentic humility is hard to duplicate.

Leaders exhibit humility by making themselves available to the people they work with. Their time is valuable, but it is not so valuable that they can't take the time to listen or discuss something that is important with others. It is very easy for people to identify leaders with authentic humility. They are the ones who return phone calls, respond to e-mails and engage with others not as a leader-to-subordinate, but as a person-to-person.

Humility is also the recognition of what a person knows and doesn't know. A humble leader accepts what he or she may not know and is comfortable hiring people around them to help fill in any knowledge gaps.

Dr. Toby Cosgrove, CEO and President at Cleveland Clinic, is a firm believer in the need for humility in healthcare leaders. He considers humility "the ultimate wisdom." Leaders don't know it all and should be aware of their own limitations. It "is not the absence of self-worth, but the validation of self-worth." (Cosgrove T. , 2016)

Empathy is the ability to mentally identify with the feelings, thoughts or attitudes of others. It is not the same as sympathy which implies feeling sorry for someone. It involves knowing people and knowing about the people you work with, especially your direct reports. On a business level, this includes understanding their motivations, career goals, education, etc. On a personal level, it includes knowing their entertainment interests, marital status, children's ages, etc. This information can be used to help establish a sincere relationship with the person which makes that 'go to the wall' moment easier to accept.

Empathy is not just for direct reports but should also be included with relationships with indirect reports and peers. Some executives like to 'walk the floors' and listen to people to get to know them especially when they start a new position. (Heller, 2017) This quality can be learned somewhat especially by adding notes to a contacts file, but that only provides a 'robotic' approach to empathy. Sincere empathy comes from the heart and is easily distinguishable from insincerity.

Leaders exhibit empathy by getting to know and understand the people they work with. They have to generally like people and like working with people to be the most effective. It is also a considered one of the requirements for effective leadership by Dr. Cosgrove. (Cosgrove T. , 2016)

Vision is being able to see things others don't see or before others can see it. People with vision can sometimes see the endgame before it even begins. The challenge for such visionaries is getting others to see the vision and gaining their buy-in. This process can be very frustrating for people with this natural quality because the people they work with, especially in healthcare, are so used to doing things a certain way and can be reluctant to make any changes. This is a quality that can be learned to a degree using decision making processes and tools, but those with natural vision can reach the same or better direction more efficiently with a better understanding of the most important variable – the human factor.

Leaders with vision can effectively chart the course for where they need to go and communicate that vision in a manner that everyone can understand. This is where the direction and inspiration comes in. Good leaders chart the course by providing direction. Great leaders make their followers feel good about where they are going.

Risk-Taking is built in to becoming a leader. By accepting the position, the leader has fundamentally accepted a certain amount of risk. The leader needs to be prepared to accept the good as well the bad outcomes that may occur. There are several types of risks the leader must be prepared for including: reputation risk, career risk, interpersonal risk and financial risk. Being at the front of the team or organization opens the leader to "arrows" potentially pointed at their back. If the leader can't accept criticism or negative feedback, maybe they should consider another position.

Leaders who take risk aren't just taking risks for risk's sake. The risk is calculated and weighed against the potential for success or failure. They must be ready to try new things when necessary and adapt their leadership style to the situation. Calculating risk is a skill that can be learned, but the nature of leadership requires the leader to accept a certain level of risk with the position.

The Mixology

The next questions most people want to ask is how many traits do they need to have and how much of each trait should be innate versus learned. At this time, there is no mathematical formula to unequivocally answer these questions, but, just like leadership, you sometimes just have to have a 'feel' for it.

Based on interviews, observations and research, the best leaders are the ones who possess, and are good at, all four traits. Some possess three traits while others only two. Even though they may not be gifted with all four traits, they may have other compensatory abilities that make up for what they are missing.

Although the best leaders have most of these traits innately, there is a room for some learning, but in most cases, it needs to be less than 40%. A person can learn some of the qualities, but there is only so far they can go with humility or empathy that is not authentic.

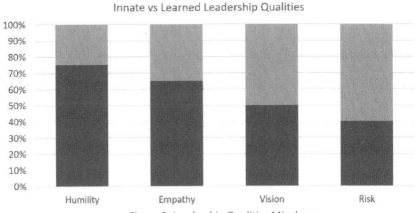

Figure 3: Leadership Qualities Mixology

Why Most Leadership Training Fails

There is a plethora of leadership development programs being offered. Most are designed to keep the participants coming back again and again. Ironically, when leadership is taught at the university graduate school level, it is completely different. It is taught as a process that is personalized to the individual with appropriate feedback and mentoring. Consequently, the primary reasons most leadership training fails are because:

- Training is skills-based versus process-based. Possessing the skills without the process only addresses a portion of what is needed to become a better leader. It's like the chef and the ordinary cook setting out to make the same dish. They may both have the same ingredients, but the dish created by the chef will usually be much better because the chef knows the process intimately based on extensive practice in making the dish.

- They use a one-size-fits-all instead of an individualized approach. Not everyone has the skills taught in the classes or can be good at them once they've learned them.

- There is no follow up or feedback loop to see if what was learned was properly implemented. This approach is contrary to that used in most academic programs and is supported by the Kolb Experiential Learning Cycle. Kolb views learning as a multi-stage integrated process with each stage supportive of and feeding into the next. Effective learning only occurs when a learner is able to execute all four stages of the model. (McLeod, 2013)

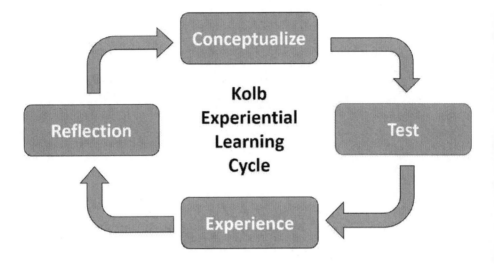

Figure 4: Kolb Learning Cycle (McLeod, 2013)

The Professional Leadership Process™ detailed in this book is designed to be learned once and adaptable to almost any situation the leader or potential leader may encounter.

Primary Leadership Influences

There are three primary influences that impact a leader's effectiveness. They are the:

- Leader – includes his/her personality, abilities and expertise;
- Followers – the Leader's constituents and is comprised of their values, norms and status;
- Environment – the atmosphere in which the Leader and Followers interact with and includes the culture, tasks, change and government impact.

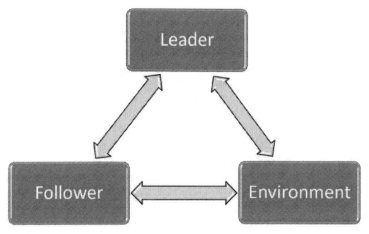

Figure 5: Primary Leadership Influences Model in Equilibrium

These influences must work in equilibrium for the leader to effectively lead. If any of the influences fall out of equilibrium, the leader cannot lead effectively. When any of the three influences exert a stronger or weaker influence, the leader must adapt to bring the model back into equilibrium. This is illustrated by the influences being the same size in the figure above.

The influences can get out of equilibrium, such as when the Leader is working with strong or powerful Followers. This can occur in working with doctors at a hospital, tenured professors at a university, professional (versus collegiate) athletes and even some volunteer organizations. All of these scenarios can make it difficult for a leader to be effective.

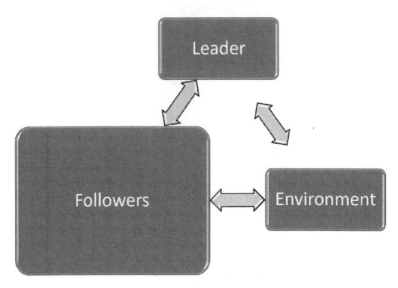

Figure 6: Primary Leadership Influences Model with Powerful Followers

The influences can also get out of equilibrium when the Leader is facing a challenging Environment. This can occur when the industry is facing dramatic changes like what currently exists in healthcare. A shift in how consumers shop has also caused a challenging environment for

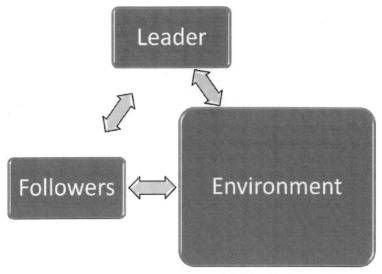

Figure 7: Primary Leadership Influences Model with a Challenging Environment

brick and mortar retailers. They either have to adapt or go out of business.

Law enforcement officers regularly face challenging situations. One minute they could be directing traffic or handing out speeding tickets. The next minute they could be faced with a domestic or hostage situation. They have to know how to adapt to the seriousness of each situation. These challenging Environments can make it difficult for a Leader to be effective.

Another way the influences can get out of equilibrium is when the Leader overwhelms the Followers and the Environment. This is not leadership in any form; it is simply intimidation. Not much can be done in this situation until the Leader becomes self-aware enough to want to change. Until then, the Leader will most likely experience a steady exodus of Followers leaving the organization and the decline of the department or organization.

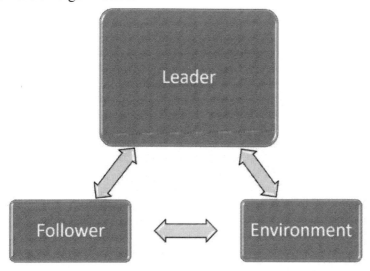

Figure 8: Primary Leadership Influences Model with an Overpowering Leader

Whatever the situation, to be effective, the leader must adapt to return all the primary influences back to equilibrium.

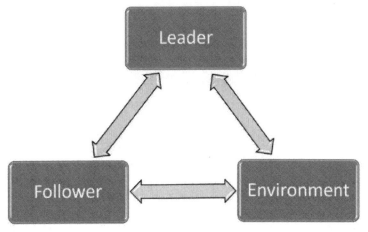

Figure 9: Primary Leadership Influences Model Returned to Equilibrium

Secondary Leadership Influences

In addition to the Primary Leadership Influences there are other influences at work that a leader must be cognizant of to be effective. Even if the leader is at the top of the organization, he or she still reports to a Board of Directors. If the person in the Leader position is in middle or senior management, they need to also work with their Manager and/or Peers. The most effective leaders are the ones that are not only adept at managing their primary leadership influences, but also handling their managers and peers. A Leader provides leadership of the Primary Leadership Influences and manages the Secondary Leadership Influences. Consequently, the total leadership influences model for any position in an organization should include all five influences.

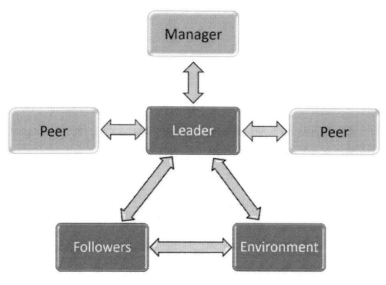

Figure 10: Primary Leadership Influences Model with Secondary Influences

"Leadership is not a skill to be learned, but a process to be refined."
- J. Bryan Bennett

Tales from the Leadership Front - My Leadership Journey

This book has been as much about helping others become better leaders as it has been about me and my leadership journey. I was one of those people considered a "natural-born" leader throughout my life. I held leadership positions in high school and college clubs. I started chapters of professional organizations in the cities I lived in and eventually rose to become president of my graduate school alumni club Chicago chapter, the largest alumni club chapter in the world for the school and the first and only African-American chapter president in its history.

When I began teaching leadership courses at the university, I had to reconcile the fact that the material kept stating that leaders are made and not born. I wondered how this could be if I was considered a leader all my life and I had never taken a leadership course. It was only until I read an article about the importance of being an empathic leader that it began to dawn on me that leaders are born and made. They are born with certain innate qualities and they are made through certain life circumstances that 'activate' those qualities and propels them to become a leader.

I related to the empathy in leadership article (Naseer, 2016) and determined it was an attribute that set me apart from others. The second attribute was vision. I don't see the world and the situation for what they are, but see them for what they could be. Once I see what can be, I invest the mental cycles into figuring out how it can happen. That is how I developed a plan to utilize barcodes in the library to track locations of books 10 years before they were widely put into use. That is how I co-developed a customer relationship marketing implementation model that was recognized by Gartner, the world's leading research and advisory company, as being one of the top visions in the industry. That is also how I developed a plan for implementing electronic data in healthcare almost 2 years before it was signed into law.

Empathy and vision were great starts, but I knew there was more. I stumbled upon humility during my conversation with Dr. Cosgrove. I was surprised by how humble of a person he was. He put the patients and the Cleveland Clinic way ahead of any accomplishments he has personally achieved in his illustrious career. After our interview, I thought about other great leaders I knew, including one of my mentors, and determined that humility was also a necessary quality. The leader must put the organization ahead of themselves which is something I also try to do daily.

Humility is also manifested in the leader recognizing what he or she knows or doesn't know. A humble leader will identify the gaps in their knowledge and surround themselves with good people with complimentary skills that in turn makes them better overall leaders.

Lastly, I contemplated what else about me made me a good leader and could I find that quality in others. That's when I arrived at risk-taking. By the very nature of being a leader, they are taking risks every day. They have to convince people to follow them knowing full well that they could be leading the team to success or failure. As the leader, they recognize there are naysayers with arrows pointed at their backs ready to launch them if they don't succeed (and sometimes, even if they do succeed). I have always been one comfortable not following the crowd. I loved the "road less travelled" and embraced the uncertainty with the certainty. That is what has made me into the effective leader I am today.

Chapter Two -
The Healthcare Leadership Challenge

"All of the great leaders have one characteristic in common:
it was the willingness to confront unequivocally the
major anxiety of their people in their time.
This, and not much else, is the essence of leadership."
- John Kenneth Galbraith

Leadership in healthcare is a bigger challenge than many realize. The industry transformation has illuminated many of the deficiencies in technology, talent and leadership. Starting with electronic medical records (EHR), then adding ICD-10, population health to ongoing hospital operations, healthcare executives have been challenged with making substantial changes in a short amount of time. It's like asking an electronics retailer to become a fine French restaurant in under 12 months.

Executive leadership is the most important critical success factor in any change management situation. It is often known as Executive Sponsorship in Lean Six Sigma or Project Management training. It is critical to making sure the needed resources are available to complete the project, including financial and personnel resources. It involves having a vision for where the organization and the team is going. Building credibility with the team members will be essential to raising them to and beyond their potential. A credible leader will be able to get his/her followers to go over and above the basic requirements of the job.

Electronic Health Records Implementation

Many lessons can be learned from the industry's experience with implementing EHR solutions. Several healthcare executives ended up on the "wall of shame" as they were forced to resign or were terminated due to problems with their EHR implementations. These stories became more frequent as healthcare organizations progressed deep into their EHR implementation cycle. A closer look revealed that the reasons were almost always the same, i.e., lack of physician engagement, difficult implementation time frames, or lack of the proper resources. Further examination, revealed that there was usually one primary reason for the failure – ineffective leadership in two distinct areas, specifically software selection and use of resources.

Many tried to blame the solution as the problem. The hindsight questions were usually, "Why did we (or did we not) purchase xyz solution?" The name of the EHR solution was really irrelevant. The reason the CEO and/or CIO were terminated or resigned wasn't because they bought a "good" or "bad" EHR solution. One of the reasons they failed was because they used a faulty software solution selection process. There are no one size fits all solutions in the marketplace. Buying a solution that is overkill is just as bad as buying one that is not adequate enough. Too much of a solution will strain your implementation resources. Too little of a solution will not adequately deliver the expected results.

The second reason many of them were fired or resigned was because of poor planning and/or management of resources. Starting without the proper internal project management and/or technical resources to implement an EHR, then hiring the vendor to perform the complete implementation or not hiring an experienced third-party organization to manage the project, set them on a course for failure. It is usually less costly in the long-run to hire a third-party project manager if the organization doesn't have the internal capacity to daily manage the implementation. Many organizations tried to do it internally only to find out they've spent millions of dollars with very little to show for it and either end up hiring a third party to get them on track or abandoning the project altogether.

Without the right support, the right resources may not be allocated or acquired when needed to help complete the project. A hospital system CEO once commented that the year before they implemented their EHR solution they had 15 data analysts. A year later, the staff was up to 50. This is a factor that many organizations overlooked when they selected their vendor. Resources were already strained by the shear cost of the EHR solution alone, which now has to add another $2 to $3 million in support staff. Therefore, the executive must take an active role in the implementation process and realize that there is a time to lead (speak) and a time to follow (listen). This support must extend beyond the start of the project as the executive needs to be engaged throughout the project implementation.

Healthcare Analytics Implementation

The Healthcare Center of Excellence (HCOE) has been tracking the healthcare industry's progress towards population health analytics since 2014 using their proprietary Healthcare Transformation Change Model. (Healthcare Center of Excellence, LLC., 2017) This model was developed in 2013 to help healthcare organizations understand the requirements to become an analytics-focused healthcare organization. The concepts were based on a previously developed customer

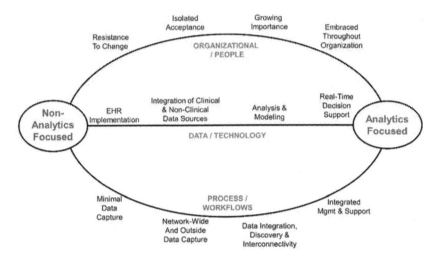

Figure 11: The Healthcare Transformation Model

relationship marketing (CRM) implementation model which was considered by Gartner to be one of the top three CRM visions at the time and has since become the basis for most successful CRM implementations today.

It is widely accepted that there are 4 types of analytics (The Four Types of Analytics, 2014), which are:

- Descriptive analytics, which answers "What's happened?"
- Diagnostic analytics, which answers "Why did it happen?"

- Predictive analytics, which answers "What may happen?"
- Prescriptive analytics, which answers "How can we make it happen?"

Therefore, the Healthcare Transformation Change Model with the types of analytics performed at each stage would be as follows:

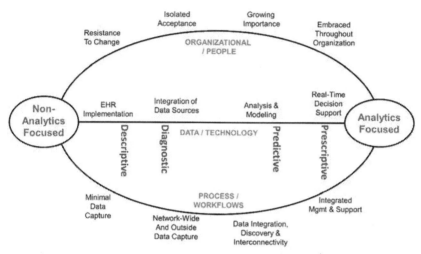

Figure 12: The Analytics Stages of the Healthcare Transformation Model

In a separate study conducted in 2015 by the HCOE, participants were asked to identify 5 challenges they faced in implementing healthcare analytics. (Healthcare Center of Excellence, LLC., 2015) The participants included people from all levels of healthcare organizations from locations across the United States. The challenges were classified into 10 categories for further examination. Those categories were:

- analytics tools
- change management
- costs
- data management
- education

- integration
- leadership
- process
- talent
- technology

The top 3 categories chosen were leadership (29%), data management (18%) and talent (14%).

Leadership included common terms/phrases such as:

- "lack of priority"
- "lack of vision"
- "need for buy-in from staff"
- "lack of direction"

Leadership comments also include phrases such as:

- "disparate EHR systems"
- "siloed systems"
- "teams not working together"

These issues can all be resolved through proper leadership.

Data management included terms/phrases such as:

- "lack of data standardization"
- "lack of data stewardship"
- "lack of definition of key variables to study"
- "where does the data reside"
- "quality of data"

Talent included terms/phrases such as

- "lack of adequate analytics talent"
- "hiring the right people"
- "lack of skills"
- "not enough qualified staff"
- "retaining talent"

Overall, the distribution of responses was decidedly pointed at leadership.

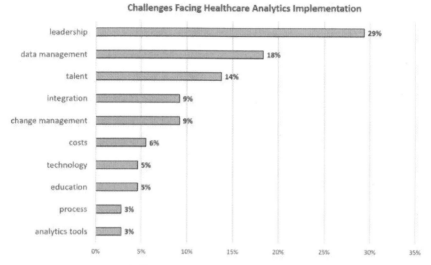

Figure 13: Challenges Facing Healthcare Analytics Implementation

Even more surprising was the source of the comments. As part of the study, the participants were asked to include their titles on the survey form they submitted. The titles were summarized into general categories which indicated the responses included all levels of the healthcare organization, from C-Level to the Analyst. The participants were divided into two groups – wide span of control, which included participants at the director level and above, and narrow span of control which included all others.

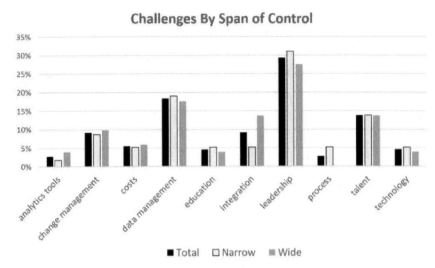

Figure 14: Analytics Implementation Challenges by Span of Control

The only challenges where the disparities were significant were in integration and processes. This is likely because of perspective. The wide span executives are anxious to see results of their investments through data integration versus the narrow span personnel desire for more and better processes to make their jobs easier.

Based on this additional information, leadership was incorporated into the transformation model. Leadership is not a continuum, but it must be present in each stage of each continuum and applied consistently throughout the transformation. It is represented in the model like a thermometer going from the bottom, low-level of leadership, to the top, high-level of leadership. It is the most important critical success factor in any change management situation and is also known as Executive Sponsorship in Lean Six Sigma or Project Management training. (Bennett, Competing on Healthcare Analytics, 2016)

Healthcare Analytics Transformation Model

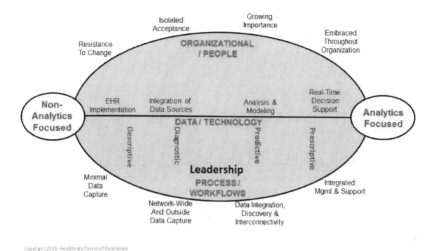

Figure 15: The Healthcare Analytics Transformation Model With Leadership

The Healthcare Leadership Influences Assessment

Based on an analysis of the healthcare industry, the leadership influences would best be described as out of equilibrium with strong **Followers** in the form of physicians and a very complex **Environment** in the form of the changing technological and economic model. The physicians account for the vast knowledge, expertise and revenue stream of the hospital. Without them, the hospital would be hard-pressed to survive. Because of their specialty expertise and their patient portfolio, many would be difficult to replace. Unfortunately, many physicians have resisted much of the technological changes, some simply because they didn't want to change the way they've practiced medicine for decades and others because of what was implemented or how it was implemented.

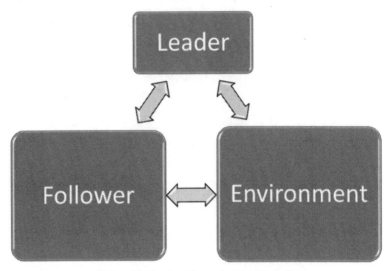

Figure 16: The Healthcare Leadership Influences

The **Environment** is considered complex because of the technological and government changes that the industry has been expected to make in a short amount of time. Many recognize that the healthcare industry is behind other industries in the use of technology to manage the business. Technology is used regularly to examine and diagnose patients, but before the widespread use of EHRs, the notes were mostly written by hand and added to a paper chart. EHRs have made it easier to safely record patient information, but it is still a long way away from complete interoperability. The design of the EHRs has also made the patient encounter more off-putting because the physician is spending so much time trying to enter the information versus engaging with the patient. Added to this is new and changing government requirements for patient safety and quality and you have the formula for a very challenging environment.

To bring the influences back to equilibrium, the leader must adapt their leadership style to become more effective. Adaptive methodologies will be further discussed in Chapter Nine, but many healthcare leaders recognize what needs to be done.

> *"Effective leadership is one of the most neglected components of quality healthcare. It's essential at every level – from large integrated medical systems, to community hospitals and physician practices."*
> -- *Dr. Toby Cosgrove, CEO & President, Cleveland Clinic*

Tales from the Leadership Front - Leadership as a Foundation

In my first book, I called leadership the foundation for implementing healthcare analytics, but in actuality, it is the foundation for everything done in any organization whether it be healthcare, business, academia or government. Without it, we are just blowing around like a 'candle in the wind'.

Imagine any building started without a firm foundation. Eventually, the structure will give way to the unsteadiness underneath it. A great example of this principle I like to use in my presentations is the Leaning Tower of Pisa. It began tilting during construction in the 12th century which was caused by an inadequate foundation from the ground being too soft on one side to properly support the Tower. The tilt continued to increase in the decades before it was completed in the 14th century. Keep in mind that the Tower didn't begin tilting immediately. It didn't start tilting when a construction worker laid 1, 2 or even 3 layers of bricks on the ground. In fact, it didn't start tilting until they began the second floor some 5 years after construction started. Because of the weak foundation, it took 3 stages and almost 200 years to finish construction.

The lesson here is that leaders can set their organizations up for long-term success or failure by the type of leadership foundation they choose to begin with.

Chapter Three -
The Professional Leadership Process™

"Leadership and learning are indispensable to each other."
- John Fitzgerald Kennedy

Professional leadership is an individualized leadership process that helps a person build a leadership strategy based on their individual abilities. This process looks at leaders as individuals. It's not a one-size-fits-all program. Everyone can't be a great communicator. Everyone can't be visionary. These people may have other abilities though that could make them a good leader.

The process begins with a complete assessment of the leader's or potential leader's personality, innate qualities and leadership abilities. Using this assessment, the program helps the leader develop their personal leadership philosophy which they must execute every day. The leader is then responsible for reflecting on how they implemented their leadership and what they could do differently next time. This information is reviewed with a coach or mentor on a regular basis to receive feedback on their performance. The leader then adjusts his or her assessment of their leadership abilities and utilizes it in the next leadership encounter. Once implemented, it creates a personalized, continually improving leadership development cycle that adjusts to almost any situation. It is the last leadership development program a person should ever need to take.

The formal Professional Leadership Process™ is comprised of five steps, which include:

1. **Assessing** Leadership Abilities – evaluating the person's personality and individual leadership abilities.
2. Leadership **Visioning** – utilizing the abilities from the assessing step to create a personalized leadership vision or philosophy.
3. **Living** the Leadership Vision – executing and communicating the leadership vision.
4. **Reflecting** on Leadership – analyzing the leadership encounter faced and how they can be improved.
5. Leadership **Coaching & Mentoring** – reviewing the leadership encounters with a peer, superior and/or coach/mentor for advice on how to improve for the future.

Figure 17: The Professional Leadership Process™

The last two steps of the process, reflecting and coaching, is what puts the "professional" in the Professional Leadership Process™. This is the same process professional athletes have taken for decades to improve on their already exceptional skills. Before and after every sporting event, professional athletes study film and use other methods to determine how to put themselves or their team in the best position to win. You might recognize it as "reviewing game film" or "working with the swing (or any other positional) coach" or "working on the game plan." No matter which sport you think of, that is how athletes prepare for a game, match or round. The studying doesn't end when the sporting encounter begins. It continues sometimes during the game or match with football players reviewing offensive and defensive sets and usually continues after the game or match.

Figure 18: The Professional Steps of the Professional Leadership Process™

Some athletes with well-known training regimes, include:

- Tom Brady is completely devoted to the game of football and to keeping his body in shape to play as long as he can. He has had the same personal trainer for the last 10 years who helps him continue to refine his workouts, push his physical and mental self. To Brady, this isn't work, it's a lifestyle choice. According to him, "Other than playing football, the other thing I love to do is prepare to play football." (King, 2016)

- Peyton Manning was known as an avid game film watcher. He would watch film before games to help him recognize the defensive alignments so that he could call the right plays at the scrimmage line. After the game, he reviewed game videos on the way home from road trips to see what he might have missed and to prepare for the next game.

Athletes aren't the only people who train like this. Other professions also utilize the learn, study, practice, review/feedback and implementation (SPRI) development methodology, including:

Physicians are on the top of the list not just because this is a healthcare focused book but because their training is unlike most other professions. They learn anatomy in medical school. Then they learn and practice performing various procedures under experienced physicians until they can successfully perform them on their own. But their training doesn't end there. Throughout their professional career, they are required to keep their knowledge current through continuing medical education and learning new procedures, depending on their specialty.

Musicians & Singers continue to work at their craft even after they become accomplished. They create songs, test them out with group members or in front of live audiences and revise them until they achieve the sound or delivery they desire.

Artists make multiple versions of their paintings or sculptures. What is seen on display in the museum or art gallery is usually just the final product. Seldom does the public see all the previous iterations the artist completed before they achieved what they had conceived in their head.

Professors continue to work at their classes. This is especially true when they are writing a new class or teaching a class written by another course writer for the first time. It takes a couple of times teaching the class before the professor believes the class clearly communicates the materials and the course expectations.

Many amateur athletes train in a similar manner, but most exercise very little power over their situation. When you compare an amateur/collegiate football or basketball player to a professional player, you will find that the professionals sometimes make many times more than their coaches or even team executives. Consequently, they exert a great deal more power over the relationship, even to the extent of getting the coach fired because they didn't get along or didn't want to play for them. The Professional Leadership Process™ is adaptable to scenarios when the followers can potentially exert undue influence or when the environment is very complex, thus it is called "professional" for this reason.

If athletes who are the top 1% of the top 1% can continue to develop their already exceptional skills, then why can't leaders. It's not about the number of leadership courses or workshops a person takes, but about finding something that works for the person and sticking to it. The key is adaptability to a given situation. If it's not adaptable, it won't be sustainable. If you take nothing else from this book, implementing the **Reflection** and **Coaching/Mentoring** steps will serve you well in the long-run.

> *"I've missed more than 9,000 shots in my career.*
> *I've lost almost 300 games.*
> *Twenty-six times I've been trusted to take*
> *the game winning shot and missed.*
> *I've failed over and over and over again in my life.*
> *And that is why I succeed."*
> *- Michael Jordan*

Tales from the Leadership Front – Sports as a Metaphor

While developing the early iterations of the leadership process, I realized how similar a personalized leadership development process was to how athletes train. The coach assesses the athlete's personal strengths and weaknesses and prescribes a training regimen that improves their strengths and compensates for their weaknesses. Additionally, their training is usually specialized for the position, opponent or environment they would be performing in. A quarterback in football does not receive the same training as a wide receiver. A first baseman in baseball does not train the same way a catcher does. A center in basketball doesn't receive the same training as a guard. The same holds true for individual sports in which the athlete's training is based on their potential opponents, conditions, track, course or court they may be performing on.

Athletics is also useful because there is a clear distinction between amateur and professional athletes. Sometimes these lines may blur, but typically, the amateur athlete is not financially compensated for their efforts while a professional athlete does. At the professional level, these athletes can exert significant influence over the team, game or match because there is a limited number of athletes that can perform at that level. At any given time during the season, each sport has a defined total number of roster spots in the league, including:

- National Football League with 1,700 players
- Major League Baseball with 1,300 players
- National Hockey League with 700 players
- National Basketball Association with 500 players

This doesn't include the number of ranked golfers or tennis players of which only the top 200 or so actually make a reasonable living. (Morales, 2013) Keep in mind that these are the top athletes in the world. Not just the United States. If the best athletes in the world receives ongoing personalized training and coaching, then shouldn't leaders who face more challenging situations and have a greater impact on the world.

I believe sports are not just a metaphor about life, but are also a great metaphor for leadership. We've already discussed the similarities in the training process, but sports also teaches:

- Responsibility - understanding a person's role on the team
- Teamwork - working with everyone on the team, not just the people he or she likes
- Commitment – ongoing preparation and continual improvement
- Humility – accepting defeat since no one is successful 100% of the time
- Self-discipline - learning to focus on what is most important

After reading this, I hope you will view leadership and sports in an entirely different light.

Chapter Four -
Assessing Leadership Abilities

"Becoming a leader is synonymous with becoming yourself.
It is precisely that simple and it is also that difficult."
- Warren Bennis

Assessing is the first step in the Professional Leadership Process™. It is the most important step because it is where the leader understands who they are as a person and who they are as a leader. This step is essential to creating a personalized leadership vision or philosophy.

Figure 19: The Professional Leadership Process™ - Assessing

Leadership Workbook

To document your leadership journey as you explore the Professional Leadership Process™, it is recommended to start a notebook to capture your work or use the Leadership Practice Workbook (available at www.healthcarecoe.org/workbook) which follows the process and includes fill-in forms to capture your leadership understanding. This workbook can be used as a reference as you explore the process and to refer to later in your ongoing development.

Personality Assessment

There are a number of commercial tools available to assess a person's personality and personal abilities. In interviews, most of the executives indicated that they had utilized multiple assessment tools in their careers, some more than once. Several also mentioned that the best insights were generated when the assessments were performed as part of a team initiative, finding it "greatly helpful in improving [the] ability to relate to team members." (Heller, 2017) Once a leader understands the personality, strengths and weaknesses of the people they work with, they can better appreciate and adapt to the differences of the staff.

Some of the more popular self-assessment tools include:

- DISC – a practical and easy to remember behavioral assessment which focuses on individual patterns of external, observable behaviors and measures the intensity of characteristics using scales of directness and openness for each of the four styles: Dominance, Influence, Steadiness, and Conscientious. The DISC model assessment makes it is easy to identify and understand a user's own style, recognize and cognitively adapt to different styles and develop a process to communicate more effectively with others. (DISC, 2017)

- Myers-Briggs – the Myers-Briggs Type Indicator® (MBTI®) personality inventory takes the theory of what may seemingly be random variations in behavior is actually quite orderly and consistent, due to basic differences in the ways individuals prefer to use their perception and judgment. (MBTI Basics, 2017)

- StrengthsFinder – The Clifton StrengthsFinder assessment helps the person understand how they are talented. It identifies what people naturally do best and provides customized results that name their unique talents. It shows how the person is special and how to succeed by turning their talents into strengths. (StrengthsFinder, 2017)

- SWOT - A personal SWOT (Strengths, Weaknesses, Opportunities & Threats) matrix is a framework for analyzing an individual's personal strengths and weaknesses as well as the opportunities and threats that they might face. This helps them focus on their strengths, minimize their weaknesses, and take the greatest possible advantage of opportunities available to them. (MindTools Editorial Team, 2017)

Whichever personality assessment tool you choose, remember that they don't cover every person in every situation. They should primarily be used to provide an insight into the individual taking the assessment. Some of them will yield different results each time they are taken as the person changes and others will stay pretty consistent. They are a starting point and the individual must decide how applicable or accurate they are. Utilizing the results of multiple personality assessments is also helpful to obtain a variety of perspectives.

If you have not taken an assessment recently, please visit www.healthcarecoe.org/assessments or in the Prescribing Leadership Workbook to find links to assessments that can be taken online.

Leadership Assessment

A personality assessment is only part of the equation. The individual must also understand who they are as a Leader. As previously stated, leadership is not a skill, so taking a leadership skills assessment is not recommended although they are offered by a number of organizations. A better way to assess leadership is to analyze leadership perceptions since how a Leader is perceived can significantly impact how effective a person will be as a leader.

For example, using a list of words that describe leadership, you would select 7 words that you believe describe you as a leader. Then he or she would choose 3 additional words that they desire would describe them as a leader in the future. Next, give the list to 2 or 3 colleagues. They can either be peers, supervisors or subordinates. Have them choose 5 words that they believe describe you as a leader. The next step is to match the words on a 'leadership matrix'. The words that match is where your perception and reality are congruent. The words that don't match, represent an incongruence in the way you perceive your leadership and the way your colleagues perceive your leadership. The last step is to evaluate the words that didn't match to determine if your leadership is perceived as a positive or negative trait.

46

Leadership Perception Matrix			
Leader	Colleague 1	Colleague 2	Colleague 3
Trait A	A		A
Trait B		B	B
Trait C	C	C	
Trait D		D	D
Trait E			
	Trait F (+)		
		Trait G (-)	

Table 1: Leadership Assessment Matrix

In the above leadership perception assessment, the leader's assessment of their leadership traits is very similar to those of their colleagues. Only 2 traits didn't match. One was the positive trait F and one was the negative trait G. Based on this analysis, the leader can consider if "F" should be a top 10 trait or just another good trait to have. The leader should also consider if the negative "G" trait is something they need to work at to improve on.

A list of leadership traits is included in the Prescribing Leadership Workbook.

"Strive not to be a success,
but rather to be of value."
- Albert Einstein

Tales from the Leadership Front – My StrengthsFinder Results

I have also utilized several of the assessment tools mentioned in this chapter to better understand my personality and my strengths and weaknesses. Like many of the Leaders interviewed for this book, I didn't find out anything about myself that didn't already know. I may have initially disagreed with the results, but after some additional thought and a better understanding of the assessment, I realized that it was actually correct.

The most recent assessment I took was the StrengthsFinder from Gallup. Based on the assessment, my top five strengths were:

1. Learner
2. Individualization
3. Futuristic
4. Connectedness
5. Arranger

Learner – According to Gallup, "People exceptionally talented in the Learner theme have a great desire to learn and want to continuously improve. The process of learning, rather than the outcome, excites them." (Gallup, Inc., 2017) I relate this to the innate quality of humility because a humble person is self-aware that they don't know everything and there is always more to learn.

This fits me because not only do I read a lot, but I look at every situation as an opportunity to learn. I learn from my students. I learn from fellow conference presenters. I even learn from my children, especially about mobile tools and apps.

Individualization – Per Gallup, "People who are especially talented in the Individualization theme are intrigued with the unique qualities of each person. They have a gift for figuring out how people who are different can work together productively." (Gallup, Inc., 2017) I relate this to the innate quality of empathy because empathy is the ability to get things done with and through people. Figuring out who people are and how they can work together is critical for the empathetic leader.

This is true about me because I try to know the people who work for me, who work around me and who I work for. This helps me to develop a relationship with them, understand how each person needs to be managed and how to motivate them to achieve the best for themselves and the organization.

Futuristic – Gallup states that, "People who are especially talented in the Futuristic theme are inspired by the future and what could be. They inspire others with their visions of the future." (Gallup, Inc., 2017) I relate this to the innate quality of vision because people who look toward the future usually develop a vision for how to achieve the future they perceive.

This is true about me because I approach life not from where things currently exist, but from where things could be. I am not satisfied with the status quo, but look at what could or should be.

Connectedness – According to Gallup, "People who are especially talented in the Connectedness theme have faith in the links between all things. They believe there are few coincidences and that almost every event has a reason." (Gallup, Inc., 2017) I relate this to the innate qualities of empathy and risk-taking because a belief in the links connecting people reinforces the desire to know who the connections are and a willingness to place trust in those connections, regardless of how risky they might be.

This is true about me because I love to connect with people virtually and in person and sharing my stories with them. This can be risky if one puts too much trust in a person undeserving of that trust.

Arranger – Per Gallup, "People who are especially talented in the Arranger theme can organize, but they also have a flexibility that complements this ability. They like to figure out how all of the pieces and resources can be arranged for maximum productivity." (Gallup, Inc., 2017) I relate this to the innate quality of vision because it is critical for a person to be capable of organizing and articulating how they will achieve a vision.

This is true about me because I prefer to organize and put the steps in place to achieve whatever task, project or vision I undertake.

If – *For Leaders*

If you can keep your head when all about you
    Are losing theirs and blaming it on you;
If you can trust yourself when all men doubt you,
    But make allowance for their doubting too;

- By Rudyard Kipling (adapted by Bryan Bennett)

Chapter Five -
Developing a Leadership Vision

"Excellence is never an accident.
It is always the result of high intention,
sincere effort, and intelligent execution;
it represents the wise choice of many alternatives -
choice, not chance, determines your destiny."
– Aristotle

In the **Visioning** step, the Leader utilizes the abilities from the Assessing step to create a personalized leadership vision or philosophy. The vision should be something that is actionable and measurable.

Figure 20: The Professional Leadership Process™ - Visioning

Therefore, it is recommended that the developed vision be documented in your leadership workbook, as described in Chapter Four.

There are two steps to creating a leadership vision. Step one is to utilize the strengths and weaknesses documented in the Assessing step to translate into a clear and concise vision. Step two is to state how the vision will be demonstrated in your daily leadership strategy.

Building a Vision

Utilizing the results of the personality and leadership assessments, the Leader can develop a vision, for how they intend to lead.

StrengthsFinder:

Learner

Individualization

Futuristic

Connectedness

Arranger

DISC:

Likes to work with people and help them (similar to Connectedness)

Combines enthusiasm and patience (similar to Arranger)

Prefers not to discipline people

Tends to look at all the things the group has in common rather than key on the differences (similar to Individualization)

Armed with this information about the Leader, he/she can translate the assessments into actions that can be executed as part of a leadership vision. A good way to start is by creating a table of the unique attributes generated by the assessments, then use action words to state how leadership can be shown through each attribute. Remember, what the Leader will do is just as important as what the Leader will not do. Some examples are in the table below.

Assessment	Action: Will Do	Action: Will Not Do
Learner	Share clippings from articles I've read for the team to understand what's happening in our industry.	
Individualization	Know the strengths and weaknesses of all of the people on my team as well as some basic aspects of their personal life.	
Futuristic		Discourage people who have new and interesting solutions.
Connectedness	Share information about myself to connect to my team.	
Arranger		Split up a team that is functioning efficiently if there are other options.
Prefers not to discipline people	Identify struggling team members as early as possible to prevent disciplinary situations from occurring.	Avoid situations that require disciplining a team member.

Table 2: Leadership Visioning Table

Leadership Vision Statement

Using the outcomes of Leadership Visioning Table, the Leader is ready to craft a leadership vision, some of which can be shared with their team and other parts that should only be shared with their coach or mentor. For example:

As a Leader, I will show my leadership by:

1. keeping my team informed of new developments that may impact our work;
2. treating each person on my team as an individual and developing a relationship with them, as possible;
3. identifying team members who need additional attention and providing it to them without delay.

As a Leader, I will show my leadership by not:

1. discouraging new and interesting ideas, but will encourage them and try to build on them to use for the betterment for the organization or group.

Realize that the avoiding disciplinary situations is covered under number 3 in how the Leader will show their leadership.

This is a simplified example of how the assessments in step one can be translated into a leadership vision. Step three, Living the vision, will demonstrate how the vision should be executed every day.

Know Your Vision

Tony Dungy, NFL Hall of Fame head coach of the 2007 SuperBowl Champion Indianapolis Colts, went as far as to name his leadership vision. He called it Quiet Strength, based on the fact that he seldom raises his voice (quiet), but everyone knew he was the head coach (strength). He wrote a couple of books and produced a video on his philosophy. In his Quiet Strength philosophy, Coach Dungy believed that he was there as a teacher. Yelling at players, like other football coaches do, was not teaching. In meetings with his players and prospective players he would talk to them in a calm voice and tell them, "This is how I'm going to talk to you. I'm going to treat you with respect. The other coaches are going to treat you in the same manner." (Dungy, 2008)

Not only was Quiet Strength his leadership vision, he lived his vision through his encounters with his players (Followers). He would tell his players that if they didn't think they could function in this Environment, then they probably needed to be traded to another team because neither he or the other coaches were going to yell at them, use profanity and be on them 24 hours a day to get them to play their best. The coaching staff was going to teach them and treat them with respect. (Dungy, 2008)

Leadership Visioning from a Galaxy Far, Far Away

One of the more fascinating, but largely unheralded, leadership vision stories of our time is that of George Lucas, the film producer, director and founder of Industrial Light & Magic, Inc. (ILM). Mr. Lucas founded ILM in 1975 to realize the complex special effects challenges for a new film he was working on called *Star Wars*. (Iwerks, 2010) The technology that he needed to create the film just didn't exist at the time.

When the studio executives asked him how he was going to do something, he would respond, "We'll figure it out", even though he had no idea how he was going to do it. That didn't deter him, in spite of constantly bucking up against the limitations of the technology of the time. In many cases, if one mistake was made, they would have to start the entire process over again, costing them time and money.

He saw the future of special effects in filmmaking and knew he was on the right track, so when an employee asked him if he could take six months off to learn the new MAC computer from Apple, Lucas obliged. He further supported his vision by creating a community atmosphere where creative people could share their ideas and contribute something to the projects. He knew they needed someone to support them and take the blame if something went wrong. (Iwerks, 2010)

As the Leader, Lucas recognized the limitations of the current technology but also knew that if he brought together some of the best minds in the industry, they would figure out a way to bring his vision to fruition. He also recognized that he needed to provide the right Environment for his team (Followers) to thrive and create. Their work led to the transformation of the film special effects industry with many films produced today containing some technology that his company is responsible for creating. They are able to "make filmmakers impossible dreams, possible." (Iwerks, 2010)

Healthcare Visioning

Visioning is not something specific to healthcare, but there are some healthcare specific aspects that must be addressed. Very few industries are as dependent on staff to generate revenues as healthcare. For

56

example, there is nothing for a hospital to bill if a doctor doesn't perform any surgeries on a particular day. Conversely, if an athlete doesn't play, the team will still be paid its share of the gate or broadcast fees. Therefore, leaders must know who the key influencers on their staff are and make sure they are on the same page and disseminating the same message to the rest of the staff they influence.

Healthcare is under extreme pressure to continue to innovate with constantly changing government regulations. The Leader needs to keep informed of the changes, either real or potential, and be ready to adapt to what may lie ahead. As Dr. Cosgrove stated, "vision changes over time. It is not a constant." (Cosgrove D. T., 2017)

"The key to successful leadership today is influence, not authority."
- Kenneth Blanchard

Tales from the Leadership Front – My Leadership Vision

My personal leadership vision may change dependent on the environment in which I am leading, but I have 3 basic tenets that I follow whether I'm working with employees, contractors, students or conference attendees, which are:

1. I will know my people. The better I know them, the better I am able to get the best out of them.
2. I will do whatever it takes to put my team in position to succeed. I have worked many a late night and crawled on several

conference room floors trying to find the error in the code or project plan.

3. I will not throw my people under the bus. If something goes wrong, no matter who on the team caused it, I take responsibility for it publicly. I will talk to the person who caused the problem in private. But to everyone else, I was responsible for the problem occurring because I was in charge.

Having a personal leadership vision will help provide consistency in the way the leader behaves in each situation and establishes clear expectations for team members to operate within.

If – *For Leaders*

If you can dream—and not make dreams your master;

If you can think—and not make thoughts your aim;

If you can meet with triumph and disaster

And treat those two impostors just the same;

- By Rudyard Kipling (adapted by Bryan Bennett)

Chapter Six -
Living Your Vision

*"A leader is one who knows the way,
goes the way, and shows the way."*
- John C. Maxwell

The **Living** step in the process is where the leader determines how they will execute and communicate his/her leadership vision. This is probably the most challenging of the five steps because it requires a person to implement their leadership vision every hour of every day.

Figure 21: The Professional Leadership Process™ - Living

There are a number of tools that leaders have at their disposal to 'live' their vision. They include:

- Communication
- Motivation
- Observation
- Empathy
- Storytelling
- Social Leadership

Most leaders tend to focus on the top 2 tools of communication and motivation. Some include observation in their toolkit and those gifted with empathy obviously utilize that tool. The last 2 tools are the ones that are not as widely used by today's leaders, but can be very effective if utilized properly. Since storytelling and social leadership are the newest tools for most leaders, more time will be dedicated to their discussion.

Communication

Leaders need to clearly communicate their vision to the organizations or the staffs they manage. In addition to communicating the vision, people need to be kept apprised of changes that could impact their jobs and the roles and expectations in the process. Communication must be two-way. The Leader communicates to the Followers and the Followers communicate feedback or suggestions to the Leader. Effective Leaders try to act upon or incorporate some of their feedback to show they are actually listening.

For this to be effective, the Leader must understand how people like to communicate. Some may prefer a more personal touch, others e-mail and others internal social media posts. Their preference could be generational, ethnicity or profession. Monthly e-mails or newsletters helps with communication, as well as, weekly or other frequency meetings with the organization, department or team.

Clinicians don't have a lot of time for extra reading, therefore it's important to keep the message short and to the point. Keeping it well organized will enable them to get the key points that impacts them the most.

According to J.P. Gallagher, Chief Operating Officer of NorthShore University HealthSystem, a Leader can never communicate too much. They need to understand that people have things they need to know or want to know. During a period of change and uncertainty, as the industry is in now, people need to internalize all that is happening. It might be necessary to sometimes have the same conversation with same audience, but all the Leader can tell them is "here's what I know today or here's where things stand," even if nothing has changed. He recommends using humor as the great equalizer. It helps to humanize the Leader, even if they are bad jokes. He finds that talking about kids is a great way to engage Followers. (Becker's Hospital Review 8th Annual Meeting, 2017)

Motivation

Leaders need to use more than raises and promotions to keep Followers engaged. These short-term strategies usually will not be effective in the long-term in sustaining excellent performance. The better way to bring about long-term behavioral change is through trust. (Cates, 2016)

The ways leaders can build trust include:

Walking the Talk – Aligning the organization's values with its policies is critical to building trust. Nothing is worse than an organization that states one thing in their policies or mission statement and behaves just the opposite. Aligning values and policies are the foundation for trust.

Clarifying Employee Expectations – Making sure everyone is on the same page is critical to the success of the organization. Employees will struggle if they are not given clear expectations and guidance. Therefore, the performance review process must be ongoing and not just a once-a-year event.

Awareness – This includes self-awareness, which is understanding how people interact with the Leader, and social awareness, which is understanding how people act when the Leader is or is not around, such as in a meeting. Aware Leaders know how to foster trust by aligning values and policies and are adept at noticing when they are out of sync. (Cates, 2016)

Investing Time in Employees – Followers are more energized when they are treated as individuals. Many Leaders fail to invest the time to know their Followers. Just knowing basic information about them like their career goals, family life, etc. will enable the Leader to better understand their perspective and be more empathetic to their point of view. It may not be easy to accomplish with a large team, but it will pay off in the long-run.

With all the changes taking place in healthcare, it is important to not lose the personal touch. By giving people a 'seat at the table', the Leader builds trust and lays a foundation for buy-in from the Followers. Several of the healthcare leaders interviewed for the book expressed this as a key point in their success. Mike Hartke of Northwest Community Healthcare recognizes the collaborative nature of working with physicians by treating them as an asset and giving them an opportunity to set forth the vision for the organization. (Hartke, 2017)

Observation

Leaders can utilize observation on multiple levels.

Interactions with the Leader – Observe how Followers and others behave when the Leader walks into the meeting room or in social settings. Every encounter matters. People are watching and can see what's going on. One of the ways Nancy Schlichting, retired CEO from Henry Ford Health System, uses this to her advantage by making sure to answer all her emails every day. For each person's email that she answers, that person tells 10 people they received a quick response and the Leader develops a reputation for valuing the employees. (Schlichting, 2017)

Interactions with Peers – Observing how peers interact with each other and with the Leader will provide valuable insight into the social hierarchy of the organization. Questions that can be answered through observation include:

- Do people mostly interact in small groups or as a team?
- Do the peers regularly defer to an individual or group of individuals?
- How does the other staff interact with the Leader's peers?

These answers will help the Leader understand the norms and social structure of the group or organization.

Interactions with Patients – In a hospital, the most important interactions are with patients. Leaders should observe how the staff interacts with patients by making rounds with them or visiting various units unannounced to observe how the care staff engages with patients.

Ethnographic research is a highly recommended observation tool that can be utilized to evaluate these interactions. It was originally used as a market research method to observe people interacting with a product or service in their natural environment. (Anderson, 2009) It can be utilized in healthcare to observe how physicians or nurses interact with patients and implemented by taking a more informal approach to making rounds to the hospital units. The Leader can visit the unit and talk to the physicians, nurses or patients while being keenly aware of the interactions taking place around him/her. A practical example of ethnographic research use was in the process study conducted by the HCOE where people were embedded in the various hospital units as technical support to observe how physicians interacted with the new electronic medical record software. The conclusions arrived at was completely different from what was expected. (Healthcare Center of Excellence, 2014)

Empathy

Empathy is considered one of the top attributes for success in today's global, digital economy by business leaders from around the world, regardless of geography, industry or company maturity. It enables those who possess empathy the ability to see the world through other's eyes and understand their perspectives. (Wilson, 2015) Empathy helps Leaders know who their audiences are and better understand what they want. It becomes especially important when working in increasingly diverse and geographically dispersed business environments. The Leader must sincerely be interested in understanding cultural preferences and the emotional and logical rationale that goes into every decision.

Success in today's world is all about establishing and managing relationships. These interdependencies require people to compromise and meet people where they are. To persuade effectively, the Leader must be able to empathize and be willing to understand, respect and implement someone else's point of view rather than forcing your own. (Ashoka, 2013)

A ten-year Harvard study revealed that "empathy is most lacking among middle managers and senior executives." These are the very people who need it most because they impact so many lives with their decisions. (Wilson, 2015)

In healthcare, Leaders not only have to manage very smart and independent people from a variety of professions, but they also have to understand the nature of the various cultures they come from. Getting to know and understanding their needs is one step, but getting them involved to observe how people work first-hand will be critical to building the relationships necessary for success.

Social Leadership

Using social media as a leadership tool can be very effective. The benefits of being a social leader include:

- The ability to connect directly to constituents and control the message they receive;
- Increasing the reputation and credibility of the organization;
- Increased brand awareness;
- Building trust through relationship building.

With the proliferation of mobile devices, communications might reach the targeted audience sooner than using the typical communication channels.

A 2016 survey by Domo and CEO.com reviewed the social activity (or lack thereof) of every Fortune 500 CEO and found that: (CEO.com, 2016)

- 60% of the CEOs have zero social presence on the top five social platforms (down from 61% in 2015);
- Of those on social, 26% are on just one network, with 35% of those on LinkedIn (up 3% from 2015);
- Of the 36 CEOs using Twitter, only 25 are active users.

Obviously, the lack of a social media presence can be linked to generational issues but there is probably a lot of resistance to change and concerns about privacy or security involved also.

Healthcare Executives Social Media Usage

An analysis of the social media usage by the top hospital executives as determined by Becker's Hospital Review (Rechtoris, 2017) revealed that of the 51 hospital CEOs on the list, 71% have some social media presence. The focus on the analysis was on the 2 most used business social media sites, LinkedIn and Twitter. Of the 71% with a presence,

- 31% were on both LinkedIn and Twitter
- 28% were on LinkedIn only
- 12% were on Twitter only

HEALTHCARE EXECUTIVES SOCIAL MEDIA USAGE

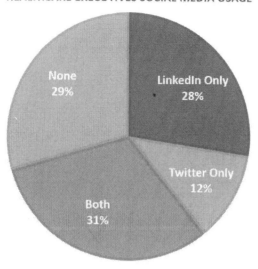

Figure 22: Healthcare Executive Social Media Usage

As the Domo.com study also revealed, LinkedIn seems to be most the healthcare executive's social media entry point.

HEALTHCARE EXECUTIVES LINKEDIN USAGE

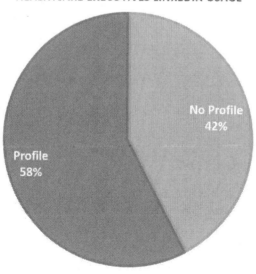

Figure 23: Healthcare Executives LinkedIn Usage

Of the 30 executives on LinkedIn, 47% of them have over 500 followers which typically indicates an active profile and 13% are LinkedIn Influencers. An Influencer is an invitation only global collective of "the world's foremost thinkers, leaders, and innovators." (LinkedIn, 2017)

HEALTHCARE EXECUTIVES LINKEDIN FOLLOWERS

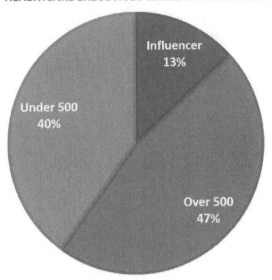

Figure 24: Healthcare Executives LinkedIn Followers

Of the 16 executives on Twitter, 31% of them have an active account with many having over 1,000 followers, which typically indicates an active profile.

Of the two social media sites studied, LinkedIn is considered the most professional with connections to the user's peers and their industry.

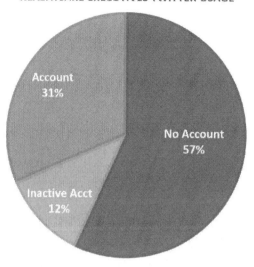

Figure 25: Healthcare Executives Twitter Usage

Twitter offers opportunity to connect with peers and the industry, but it also offers the opportunity to directly connect with employees, patients and the community. Executives who are not connecting on both

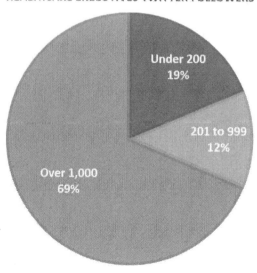

Figure 26: Healthcare Executives Twitter Usage

platforms are missing the opportunity to connect with their constituents and control the narrative.

Although it might seem like healthcare executives are more active on social media than their general business counterparts, please keep in mind that this was only a limited analysis of the top hospital executives. With over 4,000 hospitals in the country, and many of them smaller or located in rural areas, these usage statistics would probably be a lot different in a broader study. In fact, the results would probably be completely opposite with most of healthcare executives not using social media. The good news from this analysis is that most of the highly influential thought leaders in the industry have embraced the media to one degree or another.

Storytelling

Leaders need to be good storytellers because a well-crafted story resonates with the audience long after it's been told. The human brain loves stories. Think about all the family stories that have been passed down from generation to generation. Well-developed, "character-driven stories with emotional content result in a better understanding of the key points a speaker wishes to make and enable better recall of these points weeks later." (Zak, 2014) People remember stories that have an emotional impact on them. If they can relate to the hero or heroine, they are more likely to connect to the story and personalize it. Before there can be a hero or heroine, some sort of tension or challenge that changes or embraces them has to occur. That's the beginning of a well-constructed story.

Some points to remember when developing a story to tell include:

- <u>Knowing who the audience is.</u> Who is going to receive or hear the story? Make sure they can see themselves in the story.
- <u>Tell authentic or relatable stories.</u> Fabricated stories don't have the same impact as real stories because it's harder to create the details and imagery that can be derived from a true story. Stories based on a popular movie or current event work since they can be a known reference point, but there will be someone in the audience that has never seen the movie or heard about the event.
- <u>Change or conflict, not chronology is a key aspect of the story.</u> It gives the story movement by taking it from the initial problem or situation to the resolution. The more challenging the situation, the more interesting it will be to the listener. Given the story, unexpected twists pulls the audience in deeper creating an even stronger emotional attachment.
- <u>Speak to the values inherent in the story.</u> These values speak to the 'why' something did or did not happen or 'why' it is important to follow this vision. The story should clearly address the Leader's or company's values.
- <u>Test, test and test.</u> Unless a Leader is extremely gifted at telling stories, the first story they tell may not accomplish what the Leader set out to do. Therefore, it is extremely important to test your stories on small groups to get their reaction. Don't tell them you're testing a story on them, tell it when no one is expecting it and listen for their feedback before you explain to them the purpose. Refine the story and try it on another group, until it yields the desired result.

Healthcare Leaders have a variety of stories people can relate to. There are stories among physicians about how they used some new technology or procedure to save a patient who had this 'never before heard of' ailment. There are stories about nurses who went over and above to take care of a patient. Stories like these exist at all levels of most healthcare systems which can be the basis for discussions from people to technology.

Grace Terrell, former CEO of Cornerstone Health, believes in the power of storytelling and recommends Leaders "paint a story that others get excited about and want to follow." (Terrell, 2017)

Living the Leadership Vision

Here is the Leadership Vision created in Chapter Five, along with the tool(s) the Leader could use to 'Live' their leadership **[tool]**:

As a Leader, I will show my leadership by:

1. keeping my team informed of new developments that may impact our work **[communication, storytelling]**;
2. treating each person on my team as an individual and developing a relationship with them, as possible **[communication, empathy, social leadership]**;
3. identifying team members who need additional attention and providing it to them without delay **[motivation, observation]**.

As a Leader, I will show my leadership by not:

1. discouraging new and interesting ideas, but will encourage them and try to build on them to use for the betterment for the organization or group **[communication, motivation, empathy]**.

*"Great leaders are almost always great simplifiers,
who can cut through argument, debate and doubt
to offer a solution everybody can understand."*
- General Colin Powell

Tales from the Leadership Front – Leadership Lessons from a Man in a Bow Tie

A remarkable example of the use of several of the leadership tools discussed in this chapter is E. Gordon Gee, President of West Virginia University. He is known for his straightforward approach to things, his bow ties and the hundreds of selfies he has taken with students. He considers himself to be a Social CEO which is a relatively new term defined by an organizational leader who uses social media extensively.

Connecting with people is one of his great passions. He has tens of thousands of Twitter, Facebook and Instagram followers. On campus, President Gee has been known for showing up at student parties where he will socialize with students and take selfies until late into the night. How many university presidents have you seen at a student party where donations were not directly at stake? How is a leader to be heard through the vast overload of social noise that can drown out the underlying message? President Gee provides "five ways to replace social noise with real engagement."

1. <u>Humor</u>: Everyone enjoys a good laugh and self-deprecating humor leads to high viral probability as the post is retweeted, liked or shared.

2. <u>Inspiration</u>: Similar to humor, stories that talk about who you are and what you stand for tend to be shared among your constituents.

3. Photos: These show a leader is fun and approachable, but must portray the leader as who he really is. President Gee did things his way and decided that if he was going to fail, he was going to fail having fun.

4. Bragging: When you are talking about your own organization, it's OK to brag. According to President Gee, there is no need to be humble when relaying your firm's successes, innovations or impact on the community.

5. Sharing the Love: By projecting a sense of community, the leader reinforces the idea that people are part of a something larger than themselves.

Figure 27: Bryan Bennett With West Virginia University President Gordon Gee

Together these show that President Gee's use of humor is not an act, but a carefully crafted leadership strategy. By following these strategies, he is able to effectively respond to challenges at the university. For instance, after a big football win one season many students behaved unruly. Instead of waiting until Monday to send out a memo or email to the students, President Gee sent a Tweet out to all his followers stating that their behavior was not acceptable. The students responded by taking pride in their school and stopped the behavior almost immediately. This would not have been as effective if he hadn't already established a relationship with the students through Twitter as a normal channel of communication. So, it was not a surprise for them to receive a tweet from him.

In summary, people might easily confuse President Gee's use of humor as a way to just be amusing. Behind all the jokes he is a skilled social leader embracing the technology that his constituents utilize. More CEOs from universities, the Fortune 500 or healthcare systems should follow his lead to become better leaders and better communicators. (Bennett, Social Leadership Lessons from a Man in a Bow Tie, 2015)

If – *For Leaders*

If you can bear to hear the truth you've spoken
Twisted by knaves to make a trap for fools,
Or watch the things you gave your life to broken,
And stoop and build 'em up with worn-out tools;

- By Rudyard Kipling (adapted by Bryan Bennett)

Chapter Seven -
Reflecting on Leadership

"The quality of a leader is reflected in the standards they set for themselves."
- Ray Kroc

In spite of the direct links of reflection to better leadership, it is the step in the Professional Leadership Process™ that is mostly not performed at all, performed informally or performed on an irregular basis. Very few Leaders interviewed formally (written) reflect on a regular basis. Leadership reflection satisfies three needs:

Figure 28: The Professional Leadership Process™ - Reflecting

- Self-Reflection
- Environmental Reflection
- Quiet Time Reflection

Self-Reflection

Formally reflecting on leadership involves keeping a regular journal to document leadership encounters or opportunities experienced during the reflection period, whether it be daily (recommended) or weekly. In the journal, the Leader documents the leadership opportunities they experienced and answers the questions:

- What they did well
- What they could have done better
- What they had questions about

Setting aside just 15 minutes a day can help a Leader prioritize, prepare, and build a stronger team. (Walsh, 2016) Knowing the priorities is one of the most basic leadership responsibilities. The Leader must prioritize what must be accomplished and then allocate resources to get those things done efficiently. If the Leader hasn't set any priorities, how can he or she allocate appropriate resources without knowing what is most important. Self-reflection enables a Leader to understand what is most important and to focus on what could be done differently. Without setting priorities, the Leader will not know which area he or she should focus on or if they have conflicting time or resource requirements.

Preparation through self-reflection helps Leaders minimizes surprises by identifying what could go wrong in a given situation. Members of the military and law enforcement are excellent role models for self-reflection. They constantly train, forecast and plan in order to minimize surprises. Self-reflection not only helps mitigate out-of-the-blue disasters but also prepares for more routine challenges. Preparation has the added benefit of reducing anxiety about things going wrong.

Nancy Schlichting, retired CEO of Henry Ford Health System, "prepares fanatically" each morning for the day ahead by reviewing her calendar, planning for upcoming meetings and practicing for tough conversations she may have to have during the day. (Schlichting, 2017)

By self-reflecting, the Leader gets to know himself or herself better, which can lead to building stronger teams. If a leader doesn't know who he or she is as a leader, how can they lead themselves? If he or she can't lead himself or herself then how could he or she possibly expect to lead other people?

Bridgette Heller, President of Danone Nutricia (Netherlands), is a strong believer in reflecting and journaling. She believes it helps her organize her thoughts and put them in some type of order, such as, "things she can work on now; things she needs to let go and things she need to table and come back to [later]". She has found that early morning reflection works best for her, although she will sometimes reflect following key meetings or at night to clear her head. (Heller, 2017)

Strong Leaders are typically not concerned about improving their Followers. They know that if they have strong Followers, they will have a stronger team, so they encourage their teams to also perform self-reflection. Good Leaders realizes they have a responsibility to develop every Follower on their team. The adage that "if I teach them to be better leaders, they might take my job," is not a concern for strong Leaders. Their point of view is that "if I teach them to be better leaders, then there is someone prepared to do my job when a new opportunity opens up for me." Consequently, by developing a self-reflective team, they are developing a team that "has its priorities straight and arrives prepared to deal with any setbacks." (Walsh, 2016)

Athletes and athletic coaches accomplish the same with their game planning. They watch film to figure out how they can improve in their next game or match and try to find weaknesses in their opponent that can be exploited.

In March 2017, the University of Connecticut (UConn) women's basketball team lost in the NCAA semifinals to Mississippi State. This was the first time in 112 games they had lost. They had gone over 2.5 years without losing a single game. Their coach, Geno Auriemma was disappointed, but not upset that they lost. He reminded the team that this was real life. Everyone loses at one time or another. What they had experienced by not losing any games since November 2014 was not real.

Winning 111 games in a row doesn't come by accident. It's comes from hard work and dedication. Coach Auriemma prepared his players by stretching them to their limits, and beyond, in practice. They ran cardio drills for stamina and scrimmages of 4 on 5, 4 on 6 and even 5 on 8. If you looked closely at the videos of their practices, you would see, they weren't scrimmaging against other women. They were practicing against male students. By practicing against males in unbalanced scrimmages, Coach Auriemma prepares his teams for almost any situation. All they have to do is execute. Unfortunately, Mississippi State was ready for them that night and played a phenomenal game to win.

Environmental Reflection

Reflecting on the environment in which the person is leading is important to know how they should lead. As discussed in Chapter One, the primary leadership influences model has three components – Leader, Followers and Environment. If the Leader is not aware of the environment he or she is leading in, they will not be an effective leader.

The five environments previously discussed are:

- Equilibrium
- Powerful Followers
- Challenging Environment
- Powerful Followers and Challenging Environment
- Overpowering Leader

The key to successful environmental reflection is documentation in the form of identifying and listing all the influences in your particular situation. By articulating and documenting them, there is a better chance of ensuring that all influences are identified and it creates a reference to review at a later point to determine how influential they actually were.

The goal of environmental reflection is to determine which environment the Leader is leading in and to develop strategies to return the environment to equilibrium. This is accomplished by emphasizing or de-emphasizing the Leader's personal and leadership capabilities or strengths from the Assessing step and utilizing the leadership tools in the Living step. This is explored in more detail in Chapter Nine.

Quiet Time Reflection

Quiet time reflection differs from self-reflection in that self-reflection involves planning and strategizing to the day ahead or the day completed. Quiet time reflection does not include any structured planning or strategizing. It should be time when the Leader just relaxes and allows his/her mind to wander wherever it wants to go. The benefits of quiet time reflection include:

- Restoration of the nervous system;
- Help in sustaining energy;
- Conditioning our minds to be more adaptive and responsive to the complex environments people are subject to. (Talbot-Zorn, 2017)

Quiet time accomplishes this by enabling the development of new brain cells associated with learning and memory. It's like recharging (and regenerating) your overworked brain cells.

Scientists have found that real sustained silence that facilitates clear and creative thinking quiets the chatter in our heads, as well as the chatter people encounter outside all-day, every day. This mental rests allows for the mental reflexes that habitually protect a reputation or promote a point of view to take a breather. (Talbot-Zorn, 2017)

Dr. Laura Forese is a big believer in quiet time. (Forese, 2017) Dr. Cosgrove performs his reflection by limiting his work on the weekends. He then uses that quiet time to recharge and prepare for the upcoming week. (Cosgrove D. T., 2017) Dr. Cosgrove is a very busy person and his plan is a prime example of no matter how busy a person is, they can include quiet time in their schedule. Some other examples include:

1. Schedule a few minutes before or after meetings to prepare the mind for what is coming or what has just occurred.
2. Take some silent time in nature by going for a walk after lunch or before/after work.

3. Step away from media by turning off the phone and stepping away from the computer screen.

4. Take a retreat or getaway, even if it's just for an afternoon or a weekend. The break will do you well in the long-run. The getaway is good to take individually or as a team. Part of the time could be spent on work planning, but be sure to include time for social and recreational activities.

Reflecting on Living the Leadership Vision

Using the Leadership Vision and Living tools previously discussed, the Leader can document on his/her execution, as follows:

As a Leader, I will show my leadership by:

1. keeping my team informed of new developments that may impact our work **[communication, storytelling]**; *{team enjoyed the articles shared with them regularly; conducted weekly meetings to review progress on projects}*

2. treating each person on my team as an individual and developing a relationship with them, as possible **[communication, empathy, social leadership]**; *{started an internal-only Facebook page where team members shared information about their children and professional posts}*

3. identifying team members who need additional attention and providing it to them without delay **[motivation, observation]**. *{identified 2 team members perceived as needing additional attention and conducted face-to-face meetings them to determine if there was anything I could do to help them with their assigned tasks}*

As a Leader, I will show my leadership by not:

1. discouraging new and interesting ideas, but will encourage them and try to build on them to use for the betterment for the organization or group **[communication, motivation, empathy]**. *{conducted lunch meetings where team members presented their new ideas}*

> *"Being upset doesn't help you win,*
> *Doing something about it,*
> *Looking on to the next situation,*
> *Trying to make it better. That's what helps you."*
> - Tony Dungy, NFL Hall of Fame Head Coach

Tales from the Leadership Front – The Benefits of Journaling

Leaders can benefit from a regular, formal journaling practice. It is something that needs to be started until it becomes a habit. Annual or monthly reflection does not meet the need. It is something that should be done daily (preferred) or weekly (at a minimum). If it is not performed frequently, the experience can easily be partially or completely forgotten. Therefore, the review of the journal with the mentor or coach will not be as effective as it could have been. Think back to the not too distant days of paper charts in healthcare. Several physicians spent their entire weekend completing the prior week's patient charts while others completed them on the same day they saw the patient. Which physician had more complete chart notes? People forget details over time. It's human nature.

I am constantly making notes about the presentations I have made or the classes I teach. There is always something I would like to change for the next time. I have found that when I don't write it down, I don't remember all the changes I thought would improve the presentation or course. When I do capture these notes while I'm teaching or soon after my presentation, I have something to refer to before I present again.

I like using small notebooks or an app on my tablet for capturing my thoughts. If you attend any healthcare conference, you will find a dozen small notebooks from exhibitors that would be suitable to the task. There are also a lot of apps that can be used to save your notes. The advantage of the app is that it is stored online so it can be accessed from any location and it won't get lost like a notebook could. Either way, try something and make it a regular habit.

If – *For Leaders*

If you can force your heart and nerve and sinew
To serve your turn long after they are gone,
And so hold on when there is nothing in you
Except the Will which says to them: "Hold on";

- By Rudyard Kipling (adapted by Bryan Bennett)

Chapter Eight - Leadership Coaching & Mentoring

*"As we look ahead into the next century,
leaders will be those who empower others."*
- Bill Gates

The last step in the Professional Leadership Process™ is Coaching & Mentoring. It is important because without the proper feedback the Leader will not know if they are on the right track and implementing their leadership plan properly. Coaching and mentoring can be the same. The difference is that a mentor is typically a trusted person who usually

Figure 29: The Professional Leadership Process™ - Coaching & Mentoring

performs the mentoring at no cost. Depending on the organizational level of the person, their mentor or coach could be a supervisor in the same or different department, a peer at the same or different company, a high-ranking industry person or a well-respected person completely outside of the organization or industry. Any of these people could be a good mentor.

A coach, on the other hand, is someone who is usually paid to provide counseling and advice. The relationship with a "career" coach is usually more formalized than that with a mentor. They typically feature meetings at regular intervals, such as bi-weekly, monthly or quarterly. Most people will probably have a variety of mentors and coaches throughout their careers, although coaches are more prevalently used by senior level executives since it is more difficult for them to find mentors at their level and above. For purposes of this book, the words will be used interchangeably because they can both serve the same function in a Leader's career.

It doesn't matter where they're from, but it does matter that they care enough and have enough experience to provide honest feedback. Many mentor relationships begin informally with someone who has taken an interest in a person's career. The interactions can take place over a meal, over coffee or even over drinks. Sometimes a person may need a mentor to help with a specific objective, like learning about a new industry, a new job function or a career challenge. When asking someone to be a mentor, make sure to be very clear and specific about what you need and the role you would like him or her to play. Often, the mentor is not formally asked, but the relationship simple evolves from an informal relationship to a more formal mentorship connection.

Ongoing leadership mentoring has several benefits, including:

1. The mentor sees things the Leader may not see in themselves or in their leadership encounters. There is nothing better than being able to discuss personal leadership issues with a trusted person in a non-threatening environment. For this reason, it is important to choose your mentor or coach wisely.

2. The mentor helps the Leader better utilize their leadership abilities with their insights. Most people have multiple mentors and/or coaches throughout their careers and different mentors serve different purposes in a Leader's life. Some things to consider when looking for a mentor, include:

   • A person at or above your level in the organization so he or she will have a better idea of the challenges you might be facing;

   • A person in a related field, profession or industry;

   • A person who is well-connected, because if he or she are not familiar with the what you are experiencing, they probably know someone who does. (Dallas, 2017)

3. The mentor holds the Leader accountable for what they agreed to work on. Everyone needs to be held accountable for their actions and inactions. Institutions and organizations are structured in a manner that holds people accountable. Unfortunately, individuals don't always have the people around them that keep them personally accountable or have that internal mechanism that keeps them accountable in all

aspects of their lives. Everyone falls short in one way or another. A Leader or aspiring Leader needs to be held accountable for what they've agreed to work on. If the mentor suggests the Leader work on being more empathetic with their staff before the next meeting, then the Leader should come prepared to discuss the steps taken to accomplish that goal. Without a mentor relationship, that goal may be pushed off to another time or not completed at all.

Coaching and mentoring, plus reflection, are the steps that lead to Professional Leadership. You might even call them the one-two punch of Professional Leadership. It's the same process used by elite athletes and other professions for decades. In fact, there is not a single top athlete who does not have at least one coach, regardless of whether they play a team or individual sport. Some athletic examples include:

Sport	Coaches
Football	Head coach, offensive coordinator, defensive coordinator, special teams coach, quarterbacks coach, running backs coach, wide receivers coach, offensive line coach, defensive line coach, strength and conditioning coach
Baseball	Head coach/manager, pitching coach, hitting coach, first base coach, third base coach, bullpen coach
Basketball	Head coach, multiple assistant coaches (defensive, offensive, shooting), strength and conditioning coach
Hockey	Head coach, assistant coaches, goaltending coach, skating coach, strength and conditioning coach
Golf	Golf pro, caddie, strength coach
Tennis	Tennis pro, strength and conditioning coach
Boxing	Multiple coaches and trainers

Table 3: Types of Coaches by Sport

Athletes believe strongly in coaching. They realize that no matter how good a person performs, they still need someone to guide them. An athlete may see things from one perspective, but the coach helps them to see it from theirs. (Sanders, 2017) Examples from other professions include:

Profession	Coach
Musician or Singer	Voice coach, conductor, musical director
Acting	Acting coach, dialect coach
Dancer	Dance coach, choreographer
Chef (Sous, Pastry, etc.)	Executive chef

Table 4: Types of Coaches by Other Professions

The bottom line is that no matter how good a person might believe he or she is, a fresh perspective can help them improve their abilities, whether it's leadership or otherwise. This applies to Leaders and aspiring Leaders at any level of the organization. This is an area where CEOs should lead the way, but many don't. According to a 2013 study, nearly two-thirds of CEOs do not receive any coaching or leadership advice from outside of their organization, although most would welcome some advice. (Sager, 2013) This is probably because leadership is still considered a 'soft' skill by many and people in senior management positions have other items on their plates, like conflict management. The stigma of receiving leadership coaching for someone who is supposed to be the 'leader' is just too great for many, but the benefits far outweigh the risks of others knowing about an executive with a coach. In fact, coaching will probably make the more difficult tasks easier to focus on and find solutions.

Most of the executives interviewed for this book had been receiving coaching for at least 3 years. Some have trusted colleagues within the organization who are encouraged to tell them exactly what they observe. Unfortunately, the feedback gets rosier higher in an organization so people tend to tell senior executives more of what they think the boss wants to hear versus what the boss needs to hear. The key to minimizing that is to establish relationships with mentors early enough in your career so that they continue to provide candid feedback later in your career. The challenge with having mentors outside of the organization is that they can't directly observe the person. (Forese, 2017) This drawback can be lessened through the use of formal journaling in which the Leader keeps detailed notes about specific encounters to be reviewed with their outside mentor.

Interacting with the Coach or Mentor

Choosing the right mentor or coach can make or break your career and personal life. In the movie, "Indiana Jones and the Last Crusade," the Knight who guarded the Holy Grail stated after the bad guy who chose and drank from the wrong chalice, "He chose…poorly!" as the man died. When Indiana Jones chose the right chalice, he stated, "You have chosen…wisely." Choosing a mentor may not be a matter of life and death, but trying to advance your career with the wrong one could feel like it. Make sure it is someone well-respected, otherwise they won't be listened to, and someone who has the experience and connections to provide or help obtaining quality feedback.

In healthcare, choosing the right mentors or coaches to work with very independent physicians who may or may not be employed by an organization can be challenging. An example of matching the right coach to the right professional, Scripps Health implemented a physician-to-physician feedback and coaching program to improve their patient experience scores. They found that, "...the sometimes inherent resistance to change that is often encountered with new initiative rollouts, were mitigated by having a physician meet directly with key physician group stakeholders. There is inherent credibility in a trusted physician colleague who has proven clinical strength." (Sharieff, 2017)

Meeting with the coach or mentor should be on a regular basis. It doesn't always have to be on a structured schedule because things happen that can interfere. Use the meeting is an opportunity to review the Leader's reflection journal, which is why the importance of regularly documenting leadership reflections cannot be overemphasized. Without timely documentation the leadership encounter or concern may not be remembered or pertinent details may be left out that could change the mentor's assessment of the encounter.

Listen to their input for improving on future encounters and other suggestions. In addition to their career advice, they might also have some input into your personal life. If your coach or mentor never asks any questions about your personal life, then you might want to find someone else because they can't advise the 'whole' you if they don't know the 'whole' you.

Mentorship can start very early in a person's career. Often, they may be someone the Leader or aspiring Leader works for directly or indirectly. Many times, it may not be a formal relationship but be "more natural and instinctive." (Quilan, 2017) Fortunate Leaders may find a mentor or two that can guide them throughout their entire career. No matter when or where the mentor or coach is found, he or she can be very helpful in pushing the mentee to move beyond boundaries they don't realize they've set for themselves. (Heller, 2017)

The Other Side of Mentoring

It is also important for the mentored Leader to consider becoming a mentor to others in their life. Many will have the same questions and need the same advice the Leader had at the same point in his/her career. Seeing things from their perspective will not only help the mentee in their career, but also help the Leader become a better mentee. The mentee may bring up issues that the Leader had long forgotten or never resolved in their own career or life. Giving back by mentoring others helps the mentor become a better mentee because of the changed perspective achieved from being a mentor.

Junior leaders want and need mentoring too and it is important for senior leaders to hear the call for their need. (Hunt, 2017) Once someone has been identified as a potential leader, help him or her nurture their calling by giving them stretch assignments and opportunities to broaden their experience by attending conferences. (Richberg, 2017)

Coaching on Reflections

When the Leader receives Coaching on their leadership vision reflections, they can review their implementation strategies and the results they've received, such as how the team responded to the articles that was shared with them, the stories that were shared with the team and if the coach had any other suggestions. The Leaders could also discuss the content on the internal Facebook page that was created. The coach might address concerns about the kind of personal information being shared.

The Leader might be most concerned with advice on the 2 team members he or she identified as needing additional attention.

"Always treat others the way you want to be treated."
– Jerry O. Williams, former Chief Operating Officer, AM International, Inc.

Tales from the Leadership Front – Jerry O. Williams, My Mentor

I was fortunate to find a great mentor early in my career. I met Jerry Williams at a professional meeting I attended when I was in my 20s. At the time, he was the President and Chief Operating Officer of AM International, Inc, a Fortune 500 global manufacturer and supplier of printing equipment and supplies to the graphics industry. When I had the opportunity to speak with him after his presentation, he seemed to take an interest in me right away and invited me to meet him for lunch one day. We kept in touch over the next couple of years by phone or occasionally met for lunch. I never thought of him as a mentor at that time. To a newly minted MBA graduate, meeting someone at his level was a great contact to have.

I eventually worked for one of AM's divisions and was there when Jerry was named one of five business executives poised to be the first African-American CEO of a Fortune 500 company, which included his picture on the cover of the magazine. I knew Jerry as a very humble man. He always advised me to let my work speak for me and not engage in self-promotion. As much as being on the cover of Fortune Magazine was an honor, I knew it was not his preference, which he confirmed in later discussions.

Besides humility, he also embodied the other 3 innate qualities of leadership. As COO, his responsibility was to review potential acquisitions for the corporation. This involved vision to discover untapped value in the acquisition target and risk because regardless of the amount of analysis performed, success was never guaranteed. Fortunately, he had a very successful track record. He was also raised on, and lived with, strong Christian values which made it easier for him to be empathetic to the needs of others he worked with. When I would visit the corporate office in downtown Chicago, I could tell how much the staff genuinely loved working with him.

Figure 30: Bryan Bennett With His Mentor, Jerry O. Williams

I stayed in touch with Jerry over the many years that followed. When I decided to write this book, I was determined to track him down for an interview. We met for lunch and really enjoyed reminiscing about where we were and where we are now. He's retired and living locally and I'm going to make sure to stay in touch with him in the future.

If – *For Leaders*

If you can fill the unforgiving minute

With sixty seconds' worth of distance run —

Yours is the Earth and everything that's in it,

And—which is more—you'll be a **Leader**, for everyone!

- By Rudyard Kipling (adapted by Bryan Bennett)

Chapter Nine -
Practicing Professional Leadership

"Before you are a leader, success is all about growing yourself.
When you become a leader, success is all about growing others."
- Jack Welch

Now it's time to implement the Professional Leadership Process™ and make it a part of your everyday leadership journey. There are challenges with each step in the process, with some steps being more challenging than others.

Figure 31: The Professional Leadership Process™

- Assessing – This is the most important step in the entire process. The Leader must have an accurate understanding of who he or she is as a person and as a Leader. It could also be the most unsettling step in the process, as the Leader should become more self-aware of themselves. It is needed because if the Leader doesn't know who they are as a leader, they cannot expect to lead others.

- Visioning – The challenge in the Visioning step is to translate who the Leader is from the Assessing step into a leadership vision or philosophy that incorporates the Leader's strengths and overcomes or compensates for the Leader's weaknesses. It is just as important to articulate what the person will do as a Leader as it is to articulate what the person will not do.

- Living – Although Assessing may be the most important step in the process, Living the vision is probably the most challenging to implement. It involves executing on the leadership vision the person has created on a daily basis. The Leader can't cheat on this step. Whatever he or she does, must be authentic and continually show their leadership. The good news is that the Leader has several tools at his/her disposal to use. Mastering multiple tools will aid in the Leader's success.

- Reflecting – Leadership reflection is one of the most useful of the steps, but one that is least formally implemented by many Leaders. It's like exercising. Everyone knows it's good for them, but most people don't do it. Taking 15 to 30 minutes per day before leaving to go home or before starting work to reflect on the day, will return significant benefits to the Leader. Just the process of jotting a few notes down will help to clear the mind for the challenges that may lay ahead.

- Coaching & Mentoring – Although meeting with a trusted coach or mentor may sound easy, in reality, if they are any good, they will sometimes unveil truths that you may not want to hear. It is these truths that will enable the person to grow as a Leader. The challenge is finding someone to act as a mentor or coach. Early in a person's career, it's often easier for them to find someone who takes an interest in their career and who will act as a formal or informal mentor. As the person, advances, it becomes more difficult to find someone qualified enough to add value to their position. Consequently, many senior executives will seek out trained coaching professionals to advise them.

For this to be a continuously improving process, the leader should incorporate the feedback from the Coaching step to their assessment of their abilities and adjust their leadership Vision. The adjusted Vision should be incorporated and executed in the Living step and analyzed during Reflecting. These reflections should be reviewed with the Coach/Mentor and incorporated in the next iteration of the process.

Returning to Equilibrium

Keep in mind that the Professional Leadership Process™ must be applied in light of the leadership influences as discussed in Chapter One. These influences need to be identified and addressed at each stage to provide perspective as the leader journeys through the process.

- Assessing – Not only is the Leader assessing his/her own abilities but taking into consideration the abilities, strengths and weaknesses of the Followers and the Environment they are operating in. This is where team assessments can be particularly useful.

- Visioning – As the Leader is developing their leadership vision, he or she must understand the influences that could impact the vision.
- Living – It is difficult to execute on a vision without a firm understanding of who the Followers are, how much influence they exert, what Environment the organization is operating in or what are the industry or business constraints the Leader is facing.
- Reflecting – Reviewing the influences that may have led to a leadership encounter going one way or another is just as important as reviewing the encounter itself. Without the proper perspective, the Leader could engage in another encounter and yield undesirable results.
- Coaching & Mentoring – The Coach/Mentor needs to be fully aware of the influences the Leader is facing during their sessions. This perspective is critically important for the Coach/Mentor to provide accurate and useful feedback to the Leader.

Not only does the Leader need to have a firm understanding of the influences affecting their leadership process, but he or she also has to determine if the influences are in or out of balance. How the Leader executes the leadership process is highly dependent on how the influences are impacting it. There are several tools the Leader can use to adapt his/her leadership to out of balance influences.

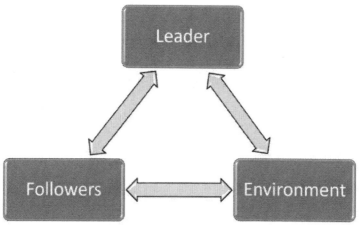

Figure 32: The Primary Leadership Influences

When Followers are out of equilibrium, the Leader can adapt using:

- Humility – Defer to the Followers when possible. Give them a seat at the decision-making table. Let them help set the agenda, but hold them accountable for the results.

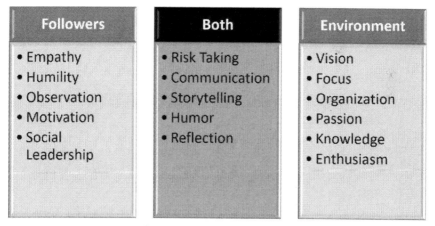

Followers	Both	Environment
• Empathy	• Risk Taking	• Vision
• Humility	• Communication	• Focus
• Observation	• Storytelling	• Organization
• Motivation	• Humor	• Passion
• Social Leadership	• Reflection	• Knowledge
		• Enthusiasm

Figure 33: Adaptation Tools for Out of Equilibrium Influences

- Empathy – Try to see more through the eyes of Followers they are leading. They might have a viewpoint that does help the situation.

- Observation – Pay attention to the Followers' verbal as well as non-verbal cues. Their body language might conflict with what they are actually saying. Observe interactions between the different Followers and Follower groups to determine who are the leaders and who could be champions to the Leader's agenda.

- Motivation – Financial motivations alone work temporarily so the Leader should utilize multiple motivational techniques. These could be in the form of competitions with or without a stated prize. For some professionals, winning satisfies the ego just as much, if not more, than a token prize.

- Social Leadership – Connect with the Followers through internal social leadership channels. Use pictures of, and with, Followers to humanize the Leader and promote initiatives throughout the organization.

When the Environment is out of equilibrium, the Leader can adapt using:

- Vision – Articulating a clear vision will help show that the Leader firmly understands the challenges the organization is facing. It should also detail what needs to be accomplished, when it needs to be accomplished and everyone's overall role in accomplishing it.

- Focus – Leaders have many, sometimes conflicting, priorities from inside and outside of the organization. Show focus for the more important priorities by conversing with the staff through e-mails, social media and face-to-face meetings. Tell them what's happening and what action will be taken by the Leader of the organization.

- Organization – Something that can destroy one's credibility is the appearance of being unorganized. If the Leader is constantly looking for their notes or a pen or their way around the hospital, they can easily lose credibility with their Followers which leads to lack of confidence in navigating the organization through the challenging environment.

- Enthusiasm – Remember the original definition of leadership includes "directs and inspires." This is where the inspiration part comes in. Inspire the organization to take on whatever challenges they are facing.

- Passion – Showing passion in the work is more internal to the Leader than Enthusiasm, which is external and inspirational to the Followers. Leaders show passion in the way they approach a challenging situation with a positive attitude.

- Knowledge – To craft a clear vision, it is critical for the Leader to have a firm handle on the particulars of the organization's performance, the industry's direction and government requirements.

When both are out of equilibrium, the Leader can adapt using:

- Risk-Taking – Depending on how dramatic the influences inequality may be, the Leader may have to take some dramatic steps to calm the waters

- Communication – Change can be unsettling to most people. Communicate with them to help them understand what the change is and how it will impact them individually. Use the technology to help distribute your message, either through an online meeting where people can ask questions, or conduct live meetings at some of your facilities and record them for access by others on the corporate intranet.

- Storytelling – Use storytelling to help people recall a challenging subject or create relatability between their situation and the story you tell. Don't make it too complex or it won't be remembered, but tell a story that is easily remembered and relatable.

- Humor – Like storytelling, humor helps people remember a situation. Use with caution if you are not known as someone with a good sense of humor. The humor has to be really good or really bad. Your audience will recall both. The middle ground is not where you want to be. If you have to explain the joke, it wasn't any good.

- Reflection – Use reflection to prepare for and review leadership encounters. Retreats are another reflective tool that can be helpful. Getting away individually or as a team helps get the creative juices flowing, enabling the development of new or better approaches to the situation being faced.

The Leadership Prescription

Based on the information and guidance provided in this book, you should now be ready to create your personalized Leadership Prescription. If you sincerely follow these steps, you will develop a personalized, continuously-improving leadership program, which should be the last leadership training you should ever need. Your leadership prescription is as follows:

1. Understand who you are as a person and as a Leader. If you don't know yourself, you can't lead others.

2. Assess the leadership influences in your situation and environment. How you lead is determined by the Followers and Environment. The Leader must recognize and adapt to these.

3. Develop your personal leadership vision and execute it daily. Although the leadership vision may evolve over time, putting that stake in the ground for what you will and will not do as a Leader will bring consistency to your Followers.

4. Reflect on leadership encounters before and after they occur. Formal reflection is one of the most overlooked aspects of leadership. Taking the time at the beginning or end of the day will provide far more benefits than most expect.

5. Find a coach or mentor to guide you through your leadership growth. Everyone needs a trusted advisor who can act as the 'mirror' by providing honest feedback on leadership encounters.

6. Reassess your abilities and apply them in the next encounter. The Leaders needs to learn from their successes and failures and adapt their leadership style to future opportunities.

"Leadership is a potent combination of strategy and character.
But if you must be without one, be without the strategy."
- General Norman Schwarzkopf

Tales from the Leadership Front – Trust the Process

It seems like everyone has laid claim to the phrase "Trust the Process". It has been used by everyone from business schools to the Philadelphia 76ers NBA team. It means that no matter how difficult the task or bad things may look, if you 'trust the process' everything will work out just fine. It's kind of another way to say, 'this too shall pass', but trusting a process that could be painful requires more commitment and involvement than just waiting for something to pass.

The phrase is very applicable to the Professional Leadership Process™. If you commit and work at the process every day, you will become a better leader. Also, remember that this is a continuously improving process, so once you get to Coaching and Mentoring in Step 5, the Leader needs to apply what has been learned in the previous steps and adapt their leadership for another cycle.

For many the Process formalizes what they are already doing, and provides a focus for every day leadership encounters. For others, it provides guidance and something to lean on to become a better leader.

Figure 34: Trust the Leadership Process Every Day!

Chapter Ten -
How Leadership is Like Golf

"The challenge of leadership is to be strong, but not rude;
be kind, but not weak; be bold, but not bully;
be thoughtful, but not lazy; be humble, but not timid;
be proud, but not arrogant; have humor, but without folly."
- Jim Rohn

Sports provides a powerful metaphor for leadership. Movies are made about leadership successes and failures of sports figures, like *"Remember the Titans"*, *"Chariots of Fire"* and *"Invictus"*. They remind us that leadership can be applied in sports situations as well as in life. When looking for a sport that compares directly to the Professional Leadership Process™, one needs to look no further than the game of golf.

Golf represents the best analogy for leadership for several reasons.

- Golf is an individual sport. It's the person versus the golf course. Even though the Leader must interact with their Followers, leadership is really the results of an individual's actions and inactions. How someone performed on the team should have little impact on how leadership is performed.

- Each golf course is different just like every leadership opportunity is different. In other sports, the field or court is the same dimensions no matter where they are played. Baseball fields might be different with larger and smaller outfields, but the major league baseball diamond is always built with 90 feet between each base.

- Every hole on every golf course is different just like every person the leader comes in contact with on a daily basis is different and has a different perspective on each situation. In fact, if a person plays the same golf course two days in a row, the course could play completely different dependent on how the cups have been moved. As in leadership, the same person could have a completely different perspective on a situation from day to day based on their motivations and other outside influences.

- Golf is played by men and women no matter their age. Leadership should be practiced by people regardless of their gender or level in the organization.

- With golf, just like leadership, it has to be practiced regularly for the person to improve at it and become more consistent. The model to improve at golf is similar to the model needed to improve at leadership, but leadership needs to be practiced every day.

Assessing Comparison

Golf

The golfer needs to assess how he or she will play the course. Some courses are wide open and some are very tight. Some have a lot of water on them and others may just be long. These courses may play to the golfer's strengths or expose weaknesses in their game. Understanding strengths and weaknesses will determine how the golfer approaches each hole on the course. If the hole has a sharp left bend to it (dog leg left), the golfer can decide to 'cut' the hole by going over the trees or whatever hazard to get to the other part of the fairway or 'lay-up' and aim for the bend and take another shot from there to the green. How the golfer approaches the hole is dependent on how he or she assesses the strengths and weaknesses of their game.

Leadership

The leader must understand who he or she is are as a person and as a leader. Success or failure will depend on an accurate assessment of leadership strengths and weaknesses. The approach to leadership opportunities must be different based on the leadership situation and environment.

Visioning Comparison

Golf

The golfer must approach (line up) each hole to execute the right shot to advance the ball to the cup. This requires imagining how to approach the hole before each swing based on his/her level of golf abilities.

Leadership

The leader must determine how they will lead each day. He or she needs to apply their personality and leadership strengths to a leadership philosophy that guides how he or she will lead.

Living Comparison

Golf

The 'Living' step in golf is how the swing is executed based on their assessment of their abilities and vision for the hole. No matter how good the golfer is, he or she will sometimes make a mistake, such as hitting the ball into the water, into a sand trap, in the rough or even out of bounds. How the golfer recovers is what separates the good golfers from the great ones.

A golfer is allowed to carry a maximum of 14 clubs in their golf bag during a round of golf. To play respectably, a golfer needs to 'master' at least 6 of them. These clubs include:

1. driver
2. fairway club or wood
3. midrange club, like a 5 iron
4. short distance club, like a 7, 8 or 9 iron
5. wedge, for sand traps or other loft shots
6. putter, for use on the green to put the ball in the cup

Leadership

The leader must execute their leadership vision every day. Again, no matter how good the leader is, he or she is bound to make a mistake, such as making the wrong decision, not articulating goals clearly, or putting trust in someone who can't deliver. How the leader recovers is what separates the good leaders from the great ones.

As previously discussed, there are 6 tools a Leader has at his/her disposal. The Leaders needs to know how and when to utilize these tools to be effective. As a reminder, these tools include:

1. Communication
2. Motivation
3. Observation
4. Empathy

5. Storytelling

6. Social Leadership

Reflecting Comparison
<u>Golf</u>

The golfer reflects on past shots or even past games. A certain shot may usually require a particular club to use, but if the golfer is having trouble hitting that club, or has never done well with that club, he or she needs to use something they are more comfortable with. It's a matter of reflecting on what worked well in the past, what didn't work in the past and what could have been done better. The golfer should also have a plan to recover from an errant shot.

<u>Leadership</u>

The leader reflects on past leadership encounters to determine what he or she did well, what didn't work out the way expected and what could have been done better. The leader should also prepare for future opportunities to improve chances for success and how to recover from an unexpected mistake or problem.

Coaching & Mentoring Comparison
<u>Golf</u>

For a golfer to become better and more consistent, coaching is needed from a golf pro. Many recommend receiving lessons when starting out to learn how to play the game the right way from the beginning, with additional lessons over the time. People tend to pick up bad habits over time or have their 'old ways' creep back into their game. Lessons with a golf pro can usually help straighten this out. Even professional golfers have golf pros to help them with their game.

113

Additionally, lessons help the golfer 'self-correct' things they my experience on the course like hooking, slicing, topping the ball, etc. They may not always be able to correct it in real time, but they know what they need to work on to improve.

Leadership

Leaders need to receive ongoing leadership coaching and mentoring throughout their careers. Coaches or mentors can help the leader see things in past situations the leader may have missed and prepare them for situations that may occur in the future. Their coaching helps them to better evaluate how a leadership opportunity was handled or should be handled. The leader may not always be able to fix it on the spot, but coaching provides them an idea of what they may have been doing wrong. The best leaders, work with coaches and mentors to improve their leadership.

Golf	Leadership
Assessing	**Assessing**
◦ How you will play the course	◦ Who you are as a person and leader
Visioning	**Visioning**
◦ How you approach (line up) each hole	◦ How you will lead
Living	**Living**
◦ How you execute your swing	◦ How you execute your leadership vision
◦ Need to master 6 golf clubs	◦ Need to master 6 leadership tools
Reflecting	**Reflecting**
◦ What you did well / wrong	◦ What you did well / wrong
◦ How do you recover from a bad shot	◦ How you recover from a mistake or problem

Golf	Leadership
Coaching	**Coaching**
∘ Receive lessons from the golf pro	∘ Receive leadership coaching and mentoring

Table 5: How Golf is Like Leadership Summary

A Golf Pro's Perspective

The golf analogy was developed several months before Certified PGA Professional Geoff Tollefson was interviewed. His perspective on golf is as a player who has participated in many national golf tournaments and as a golf instructor who oversees golf instruction for multiple golf courses. He was chosen for the interview because of his teaching philosophy of "swinging as a natural movement that is unique to each individual" (Private Lessons, 2017), which is very similar to the individualized approach to leadership development.

According to Tollefson, the golf swing is a habit that takes over 10,000 swings to achieve. He realizes that the average person does not have time to practice 10,000 swings so his approach is to take their natural swing and build upon that without overhauling their entire swing. He believes the person needs to see results in their game otherwise they may give up and go back to their old ways. When people continually see progress, they tend to keep involved in the game through practicing and playing. (Tollefson, 2017)

Professional Leadership development takes the same individualized approach. You can't tell people to be something they aren't or do something they can't. It must be a process that builds upon their innate abilities that must be practiced every day until it becomes a habit.

When Tollefson teaches golf, it is important for him to understand the trainee's perspective. Do they have any physical limitations? What are their expectations, i.e. to play better in an upcoming outing or getting multiple lessons for long-term improvement? What are they trying to execute or do and where do they need to be?

Just like leadership, coaching is important at all levels of golf. A person needs someone to objectively give advice. The caveat is whether or not the person will accept the advice. (Tollefson, 2017)

"Leadership is an ever-evolving position."
- Mike Krzyzewski, Head Coach, Duke University Men's Basketball

Tales from the Leadership Front – Life Imitating Art in Leadership

I was invited to speak at the Oregon Association of Hospitals and Health Systems (OAHHS) annual retreat in July 2017 in Bend, Oregon. The presentation was on my foundational approach to implementing healthcare analytics which included a discussion of the importance of leadership. This was based on the study previously discussed in Chapter Two that leadership was the top challenge to implementing healthcare analytics. Not data. Not talent. Not technology. But leadership. As part of the leadership discussion was the 5-step Professional Leadership Process™ that culminates with reflecting and coaching.

I ended the session with this comparison of how leadership is like golf. Each day, the leader faces new challenges just like each golf course is different and every hole on every course is different. As a leader must reflect on how to address each leadership encounter, the golfer must reflect on how he or she played the previous hole or course. To improve, the golfer usually seeks help from a golf pro to work out problems in their game. In leadership, the leader should get advice from a trusted coach or mentor to help him/her become better leaders.

In addition to my speaking and participation in a panel discussion on healthcare analytics, I was also invited to participate in their golf outing. I didn't consider that a problem when I booked the event four months earlier, but with my travel schedule for other speaking engagements and writing this book, didn't provide time for me to work on my golf game. Therefore, on the weekend before the trip, my son and I went to the driving range to get some swings in. I figured that if I at least knew what a golf ball looked like, I wouldn't embarrass myself too much. Well my son did pretty well, but I was terrible. I was never a great golfer even when I played regularly, but I could usually hold my own. That afternoon, I couldn't hit a drive straight or for any distance and couldn't figure out what I was doing wrong based on the knowledge I had accumulated from previous golf lessons. I went home frustrated and decided to call the golf pro I recently interviewed to see if I could work in an emergency session the next morning. Unfortunately, he was working a golf outing the 2 days before I was supposed to leave for my trip and couldn't fit me in.

When I got to Bend, I warned people that I hadn't had much practice and asked them not to be too frustrated with me. At least the outing was 4-person best ball, otherwise, I'd probably still be on the course.

I stepped up to the first tee and it finally dawned on me what I had been doing wrong at the driving range. I focused on my swing and hit the ball straight about 150 yards. This went on for the rest of the afternoon. I even took second place on the 179 yards closest to the pin hole (I came within 6 feet of the pin and was beat by 2 feet). If it hadn't been for my reflecting on what I was doing wrong and the ability to correct that based on my previous lessons, it would have been a very frustrating afternoon. Instead, I had a great time and my foursome used many of my shots. My short game still needs a lot of work, but that requires a lot more touch and practice, but otherwise, I was happy with how it turned out.

Figure 35: Life Imitating Art in Leadership

This was a clear case of life (my golf game) imitating art (my leadership presentation). Knowing who you are as a leader, just like knowing who you are as a golfer, can lead to much success with regular reflection and coaching.

Chapter Eleven -
Closing Thoughts on Professional Leadership

"I've learned that people will forget what you said,
people will forget what you did,
but people will never forget how you made them feel."
- Maya Angelou

Hopefully, by now, I have effectively made the case for why the Professional Leadership Process™ is a superior approach to developing leaders. Leadership development must be individualized and based on the person's capabilities. Reflection and coaching are critical to the success of the leader. Without proper coaching, a leader will not improve. The main differences are summarized as:

Typical Leadership Programs	Professional Leadership Program
Skills focused	Capabilities focused
One size fits all	Individualized program
No feedback loop to see if training implemented properly	Reflection and Coaching feedback is an essential part of program

Table 6: Leadership Program Comparison

Leadership Challenges

Leadership has many challenges and it is crucial for the Leader to recognize and be ready to adapt to these challenges if he or she is to lead. Some things to remember as you undertake your leadership journey, include:

1. <u>Leadership takes vision</u>. This concept has been discussed throughout the book. A Leader is able to see things others can't see or before others see them. Many times, a Leader has to use incomplete information in making decisions. A Leader needs to trust gut feelings based on the available information and prior experience.

2. <u>Leadership is hard and risky</u>. There is a high-degree of risk involved in making decisions based on incomplete information. That's why Leaders must seek and listen to the advice of others and get feedback through coaching and mentoring.

3. <u>Leaders need determination</u>. Leaders will not be effective if easily swayed by the crowd or public opinion. They must be driven and stay focused on the challenges ahead and possess their own internal compass. A misguided Leader is like driving on an expressway without exit ramps. The Leader keeps going but never reaches a destination or completes a task/project. Leadership does not happen overnight, but it needs to have the Leader's attention and be practiced every day.

4. <u>Leaders have to be team players</u>. The first challenge is to recognize that they are part of several teams and the second is to find their role in the teams. In some situations, they have to lead and in others, they may be more effective by following. Leaders must put others first to become first and have empathy for others. Demonstrating team playing helps strengthen the commitment of the entire team. It is not difficult for people to see who really wields the power in the room. That is why humility is an essential

quality for good leadership. Empower others to be their best and communicate with others above, below and at the same level.

5. <u>Leaders need to be ethical</u>. We all have our biases. No matter what '-ism' it is, studies have proven that we all suffer from one or more of them. (Project Implicit: Education, 2017) Leaders have to remember that they are there to lead ALL the people. Therefore, it is critical to recognize what bias you might have and how it could impact your decision making.

6. <u>Leading other Leaders takes time, energy and resources</u>. Good leaders are hard to find because they are few and far between. They are even harder to keep. Leading other Leaders makes the task even more challenging. If you are leading other Leaders, it is important to stay ahead of them and keep them engaged so that they can keep adding value to the organization. Leaders are also hard to gather because they all want to go their own way. For young people who want to get leadership experience, a good place to start is a volunteer leadership role with a not-for-profit organization. The challenges are immense when you lead other volunteers, especially when they are strong-willed professionals like business leaders or physicians. It's like trying to herd butterflies. If you can lead volunteers, you can lead anyone.

7. <u>Leadership is a continuous learning process</u>. It is not a destination, but should be viewed as a journey. It's a journey that incorporates a lifetime of learnings from experiences, workshops, books and mentors to help them develop and implement their leadership strategy.

J. P. Gallagher, COO of NorthShore University HealthSystem, reminds us that credibility is part of the currency used by a leader. There are things the leader knows, things the leader doesn't know and things the leader knows, but can't disclose. The Leader will need to draw on relationships with Followers through a sense of shared destiny that is built off leading people through challenging times. (Becker's Hospital Review 8th Annual Meeting, 2017)

Practice Every Day

If you haven't figured it out yet, the key to leadership development is practicing it every day. It's just something you have to consciously work at to be better. The leaders and champion athletes featured in this book all agree.

> "You have to treat [leadership] like an [ability] you acquire and
> you must keep honing it and keep it updated. It's something
> you have to keep growing and paying attention to with periodic
> assessments."
> – Dr. Laura Forese, COO, New York-Presbyterian Hospital
> (Forese, 2017)

> "Good leaders serve the people as much as the business. They
> remove barriers and enable organizational growth and success.
> They inspire the organization to achieve an ambition they did
> not know or believe possible."
> – Bridgette Heller, President, Danone Nutricia - Netherlands
> (Heller, 2017)

"There will always be people faster or stronger than you. Work hard every day. Don't let anyone out work you. That's a choice." – Marcus Allen, NFL Hall of Fame Running Back & SuperBowl Champion (Becker's ASC Review, 2017)

"Leaders have to influence with more than knowledge. They need to build relationships. They have to coach [their followers] and inspire them." - Geoff Tollefson, Certified PGA Professional (Tollefson, 2017)

Professional Leadership in Practice

Most of the healthcare and business leaders interviewed are already following the Professional Leadership Process™ to one degree or another. All of them have taken at least one of the various personality assessments. When asked if they had a leadership vision, all of them were able to clearly articulate a vision without hesitation. This is in spite of the fact that they did not receive any of the questions before the interview. Following the leadership vision, they were able to easily discuss how they utilized their vision in their leadership every day. All of the leaders either had a coach and/or a mentor they worked with on a regular basis.

The one area where many of the leaders departed from the process was in reflection. Although most admit to performing some form of reflection, only a couple of them actively engage in any formal journaling. Basic reflection is helpful, but articulating them not only provides a means to return to them at a later date, but also helps the leader in their thought process as they articulate their thoughts. It's like exercising. We all know it's good for us, we just have to make the time to do it. Formal reflection is the biggest challenge for most leaders, but it could also be one of the most beneficial.

Process Step	% Followed
Assessing	100%
Visioning	100%
Living	100%
Reflection	66%
Coaching & Mentoring	100%

Table 7: Professional Leadership in Practice

Healthcare Leadership Challenges

Providing leadership in healthcare comes with its own set of challenges. During challenging times like the healthcare industry is currently facing, people need stability and consistency from their Leaders. Strong Leaders are needed with the courage to make the tough calls and put the patient and the organization first. Today's healthcare Leaders must have a clear vision of where the organization is going and be able to communicate that vision to whichever audience they are engaging with, whether it be the front-line staff or the medical staff. (Forese, 2017)

The Environment the industry is in is going to continue to change. Effective leaders recognize this and are prepared to adapt how they lead. Even a leadership vision may have to change over time and should not be considered a constant. Adaptability is the only constant. (Cosgrove D. T., 2017)

Size is no guarantee of success. In the initial conclusions to the 2016 State of Population Health Analytics Study, it was thought that the hospitals succeeding at implementing healthcare analytics were the larger, better funded ones. (Healthcare Center of Excellence, LLC., 2017) Upon further review, it was concluded that it was the larger hospitals, with good leadership, that were seeing success as there are a number of larger institutions that are still struggling with implementing analytics. If you recall the Challenges to Implementing Healthcare Analytics Study, respondents at all levels of the organization identified leadership issues as the biggest challenge. (Healthcare Center of Excellence, LLC., 2015) Until these leaders become self-aware of the gaps in their expertise and respect those with different talent training, (Cosgrove T. , 2016) their leadership, their organizations and their patient care will be less than optimal.

We all have to be mindful that the most important responsibility of a Leader is to serve. This is true whether it is serving Followers, serving peers, serving those above us or most importantly, serving patients. Everything a Leader does has to be viewed in the light of service. Even if the Leader doesn't view it that way, the people around him/her will. Make that commitment to serve today to become a better leader tomorrow.

"What you do has far greater impact than what you say."
- Stephen Covey

Chapter Twelve -
"If" For Leaders

You have probably noticed the stanzas from the inspirational poem "If" interspersed throughout the book. Even though it only has thirty-two lines in four stanzas, it is a very powerful poem that still resonates today.

The poem was originally published in 1909 in a collection of Rudyard Kipling's poetry and short-story fiction. It was written in the form of paternal advice to the poet's son, but the inspiration for the poem was the actions of the leader of a failed military raid. The poem is very inspirational, motivational and provides a 'set of rules' for adult living. It contains "mottos and maxims for life, and serves as a blueprint for personal integrity, behavior and self-development." (Chapman, 2017) Its maxims are still as relevant today as when Kipling originally wrote it.

Two of the lines, 'If you can meet with triumph and disaster and treat those two imposters just the same' appear above the players entrance to the Centre Court at Wimbledon; a reflection of the poem's timeless and inspiring quality.

I discovered this poem in high school. It has been a part of my life ever since. Having never been one to follow the crowd, I faced my share of 'triumphs and disasters' in my lifetime. I have even adapted this poem for my children when they were facing challenging times in their lives. When I began writing this book on leadership, I could think of no other way to finish it but with a complete adapted version of the poem for leaders.

If— *For Leaders*

- By Rudyard Kipling (adapted by J. Bryan Bennett)

If you can keep your head when all about you

    Are losing theirs and blaming it on you;

If you can trust yourself when all men doubt you,

    But make allowance for their doubting too;

If you can wait and not be tired by waiting,

    Or, being lied about, don't deal in lies,

Or, being hated, don't give way to hating,

    And yet don't look too good, nor talk too wise;

If you can dream—and not make dreams your master;

    If you can think—and not make thoughts your aim;

If you can meet with triumph and disaster

    And treat those two impostors just the same;

If you can bear to hear the truth you've spoken

    Twisted by knaves to make a trap for fools,

Or watch the things you gave your life to broken,

    And stoop and build 'em up with worn-out tools;

If you can make one heap of all your winnings
   And risk it on one turn of pitch-and-toss,
And lose, and start again at your beginnings
   And never breathe a word about your loss;
If you can force your heart and nerve and sinew
   To serve your turn long after they are gone,
And so hold on when there is nothing in you
   Except the Will which says to them: "Hold on";

If you can talk with crowds and keep your virtue,
   Or walk with kings—nor lose the common touch;
If neither foes nor loving friends can hurt you;
If all people count with you, but none too much;
If you can fill the unforgiving minute
With sixty seconds' worth of distance run —
   Yours is the Earth and everything that's in it,
And—which is more—you'll be a **Leader**, for everyone!

Figures and Diagrams

Tables

References

Anderson, K. (2009, March). *Ethnographic Research: A Key to Strategy.* Retrieved from Harvard Business Review: https://hbr.org/2009/03/ethnographic-research-a-key-to-strategy

Ashoka. (2013, May 30). *Why Empathy is the Force That Moves Business Forward.* Retrieved from Forbes.com: https://www.forbes.com/sites/ashoka/2013/05/30/why-empathy-is-the-force-that-moves-business-forward/#2b3b3a18169e

Becker's ASC Review. (2017). Keynote - Marcus Allen. *Becker's ASC Review 15th Annual Spine, Orthopedic and Pain Management-Driven ASC Conference & The Future of Spine.* Chicago: Becker's ASC Review.

Becker's Hospital Review 8th Annual Meeting. (2017, April 17). Impactful Moments and Efforts: Culture and Leadership in Times of Transforming a Health System. *8th Annual Meeting.* Chicago, Illinois, USA: Becker's Hospital Review.

Bennett, J. B. (2015, June 15). *Social Leadership Lessons from a Man in a Bow Tie.* Retrieved from LinkedIn: https://www.linkedin.com/pulse/social-leadership-lessons-from-man-bow-tie-bennett-mba-cpa-lssgb

Bennett, J. B. (2016). *Competing on Healthcare Analytics.* Buffalo Grove: Healthcare Center of Excellence, LLC.

Carlucci, R. (2016, January 19). *A 10-Year Study Reveals What Great Executives Know and Do.* Retrieved from Harvard Business Review: www.hbr.org

Cates, K. (2016, January 4). *Five Ways to Motivate Employees.* Retrieved from Kellogg Insight: http://insight.kellogg.northwestern.edu/article/five-ways-to-motivate-employees

CEO.com. (2016). *2016 Social CEO Report.* Retrieved from Domo.com: https://www.domo.com/learn/2016-social-ceo-report

Chapman, A. (2017, July 27). *if-rudyard kipling.* Retrieved from Businessballs: http://www.businessballs.com/ifpoemrudyardkipling.htm

Cosgrove, D. T. (2017, January 30). Chief Executive Officer and President, Cleveland Clinic. (J. B. Bennett, Interviewer)

Cosgrove, T. (2016, July 7). *Medical Leadership Calls for Humility, Self-Awareness.* Retrieved from LinkedIn.com: https://www.linkedin.com/pulse/medical-leadership-calls-humility-self-awareness-toby-cosgrove

Dallas, H. J. (2017, June 7). *Mentors: When you Need Them and How to Choose Them.* Retrieved from LinkedIn.com: https://www.linkedin.com/pulse/mentors-when-you-need-them-how-choose-h-james-dallas

DISC. (2017, May 5). Retrieved from Assessments 24x7: https://www.assessments24x7.com/disc.asp

Dungy, T. (Director). (2008). *Tony Dungy On Winning With Quiet Strength* [Motion Picture].

Forese, D. L. (2017, May 13). Chief Operating Officer, New York-Presbyterian Hospital. (J. B. Bennett, Interviewer)

Gallup, Inc. (2017, February 8). *Clifton StrengthsFinder Themes.* Retrieved from Gallup Strengths Center: https://www.gallupstrengthscenter.com/

Hartke, M. (2017, March 13). Chief Operating Officer, Northwest Community Healthcare. (J. B. Bennett, Interviewer)

Healthcare Center of Excellence. (2014). *Process: The Neglected Continuum in Healthcare.* Buffalo Grove: Healthcare Center of Excellence, LLC.

Healthcare Center of Excellence, LLC. (2015). *Challenges to Implementing Healthcare Analytics.* Buffalo Grove: Healthcare Center of Excellence, LLC.

Healthcare Center of Excellence, LLC. (2017). *2016 State of Population Health Analytics.* Buffalo Grove: Healthcare Center of Excellence.

Heller, B. (2017, March 12). President, Danone Nutricia - Netherlands. (J. B. Bennett, Interviewer)

Hunt, M. (2017, February 7). CEO & President, St. Vincent's Health Partners, Inc. (J. B. Bennett, Interviewer)

Iwerks, L. (Director). (2010). *Industrial Light & Magic: Creating the Impossible* [Motion Picture].

King, P. (2016, February 17). *Tom Brady Opens Up: 'I'm Not Going to Give Away My Power'.* Retrieved from MMQB with Peter King: http://mmqb.si.com/mmqb/2017/02/15/tombradymontanapart2nflpatriotspeterking

LinkedIn. (2017). *LinkedIn Influencer.* Retrieved from LinkedIn.com: https://www.linkedin.com/help/linkedin/answer/49650

MBTI Basics. (2017, May 5). Retrieved from The Myers & Briggs Foundation: http://www.myersbriggs.org/my-mbti-personality-type/mbti-basics/

McLeod, S. (2013). *Kolb-Learning Styles.* Retrieved from Simply Psychology: www.simplypsychology.org/learning-kolb.html

136

MindTools Editorial Team. (2017, May 5). *Personal SWOT Analysis*. Retrieved from MindTools: https://www.mindtools.com/pages/article/newTMC_05_1.htm

Morales, M. (2013, August 26). *How The 92nd-Ranked Tennis Player In The World Earns A Comfortable Living*. Retrieved from Forbes.com: https://www.forbes.com/sites/miguelmorales/2013/08/26/aces-into-assets-how-michael-russell-has-made-a-profitable-career-in-the-demanding-world-of-pro-tennis/#48dc42374754

Naseer, T. (2016, November 8). *The Growing Importance of Empathy in Leadership Today*. Retrieved from Tanveer Naseer: https://www.tanveernaseer.com/the-growing-importance-of-empathy-in-leadership-today/

Private Lessons. (2017, 07 25). Retrieved from The Arboretum Club: http://www.arboretumgolf.com/private-lessons/

Project Implicit: Education. (2017, 07 28). Retrieved from Project Implicit: https://implicit.harvard.edu/implicit/education.html

Quilan, L. (2017, March 25). Global CIO, Deloitte & Touche. (J. B. Bennett, Interviewer)

Rechtoris, L. D. (2017, March 24). *100 great healthcare leaders to know | 2017*. Retrieved from Becker's Hospital Review: http://www.beckershospitalreview.com/lists/103-great-healthcare-leaders-to-know-2017.html

Richberg, G. (2017, February 7). Administrator, Pacific Rim Outpatient Surgery Center. (J. B. Bennett, Interviewer)

Sager, I. (2013, August 5). *Top Athletes Use Coaches. Why Don't CEOs?* Retrieved from Bloomberg: https://www.bloomberg.com/news/articles/2013-08-05/top-athletes-use-coaches-dot-why-don-t-ceos

Sanders, T. (2017, February 22). NFL Running Back (Retired), 1985 SuperBowl Champion Chicago Bears. (J. B. Bennett, Interviewer)

Schlichting, N. (2017, May 12). Former CEO, Henry Ford Health System. (J. B. Bennett, Interviewer)

Sharieff, G. (2017, September 6). *Physician-Led Coaching to Improve Patient Experience Scores*. Retrieved from NEJM Catalyst: http://catalyst.nejm.org/physician-led-coaching/

StrengthsFinder. (2017, May 5). Retrieved from GALLUP Strengths Center: https://www.gallupstrengthscenter.com/

Talbot-Zorn, J. &. (2017, March 17). *The Busier You Are, the More You Need Quiet Time.* Retrieved from Harvard Business Review: https://hbr.org/2017/03/the-busier-you-are-the-more-you-need-quiet-time

Terrell, G. (2017, February 14). former President & Chief Executive Officer, Cornerstone Health Care. (J. B. Bennett, Interviewer)

The Four Types of Analytics. (2014, August 6). Retrieved from CI&T: http://www.ciandt.com/card/four-types-of-analytics-and-cognition

Tollefson, G. (2017, June 28). Certified PGA Professional. (J. B. Bennett, Interviewer)

Walsh, D. &. (2016, December 6). *How Self-Reflection Can Make You a Better Leader.* Retrieved from Kellogg Insight: https://insight.kellogg.northwestern.edu/article/how-self-reflection-can-make-you-a-better-leader

Wilson, I. E. (2015, September 21). *Empathy is Still Lacking in the Leaders Who Need it Most.* Retrieved from Harvard Business Review: https://hbr.org/2015/09/empathy-is-still-lacking-in-the-leaders-who-need-it-most

Zak, P. J. (2014, October 28). *Why Your Brain Loves Good Storytelling.* Retrieved from Harvard Business Review: https://hbr.org/2014/10/why-your-brain-loves-good-storytelling

About the Author

J. Bryan Bennett is the Executive Director of the Healthcare Center of Excellence (healthcarecoe.org) where he researches and advises on transformation issues for healthcare provider organizations. He is the author of the *Competing on Healthcare Analytics: The Foundational Approach to Population Health Analytics* and the "Data Stewardship" chapter for the book *ADAPTIVE Health Management Information Management* and has been published in many other journals and blogs. Some of the research the Center has completed include:

- Process - The Neglected Continuum in Healthcare (2014)
- Challenges to Implementing Healthcare Analytics (2015)
- State of Population Health Analytics (Ongoing since 2014)

Mr. Bennett is also a predictive analytics subject matter expert, predictive analytics course writer and an adjunct faculty member for Northwestern University's School of Professional Studies. He is responsible for the development and teaching of online and classroom predictive analytics courses for the international and domestic markets as well as undergraduate business courses. As an Adjunct Professor at Judson University he has taught and mentored organizational leadership graduate students and teaches marketing, healthcare marketing and consumer behavior courses at the graduate and undergraduate levels as an Adjunct Professor for other universities.

As a data analytics consultant, Mr. Bennett performed the analysis that led to the introduction of Rogaine for Women and created the organization design for Microsoft's first internal global analytics group. He has over 30 years of experience helping companies such as Chase, BellSouth, Conseco Insurance and State Farm Insurance implement analytics-based customer relationship marketing solutions. His work has been recognized by Gartner and he authored the whitepaper "A Customer-Centric Approach to Community Bank Growth" published in Capco's Journal of Financial Transformation. This whitepaper was one of 18 papers selected from the almost 200 submissions from scholarly and business leaders from around the world.

Mr. Bennett resides in the Chicago area and is the proud father of 2 teenagers. In addition to teaching, and consulting, he loves writing science fiction, golfing and college basketball.

Made in the USA
Columbia, SC
19 February 2018